A WESTERN HORSEMAN

HELPFUL HINTS
FOR
HORSEMEN

A Collection of "Here's How" Tips in One Handy Reference Guide

Compiled by
Kathy Swan and Karan Miller

HELPFUL HINTS FOR HORSEMEN

Published by
Western Horseman

3850 N. Nevada Ave.
Box 7980
Colorado Springs, CO 80933-7980

www.westernhorseman.com

Design, Typography and Production
Western Horseman
Colorado Springs, Colorado

Cover Photograph by
Robert Dawson
www.dawsonphotography.com

Printing
Vision Graphics
Loveland, Colorado

©2002 by *Western Horseman*
a registered trademark of
Morris Communications Corporation
725 Broadway
Augusta, GA 30901
All rights reserved
Manufactured in the United States of America

First Printing: November 2002

ISBN 1-58574-711-4

INTRODUCTION

THE SUBJECT MATTER OF THIS BOOK — ways to make living with horses better — has had a long and rich history with *Western Horseman* magazine. It goes back 50 years to the first *Horseman's Scrapbook*, a collection of tips compiled and illustrated by the late, great Randy Steffen. A writer, artist, historian and life-long horseman, Steffen approached the magazine with the idea of publishing helpful hints — many of them originating from his vast horsemanship experience, but many others furnished by *Western Horseman* readers eager to share their solutions to common horse-owner problems.

The idea took flight and every month for decades the magazine depicted handy tips with Steffen's characteristic pen-and-ink drawings. When readers contacted the magazine looking for specific hints they couldn't find in past issues, it became apparent that a book containing the ideas would be a great service to horse people.

Thus, *Horseman's Scrapbook* was born. There have been four versions — the last was copyrighted in 1986 — and each has topped our best-sellers list.

Over the years, however, many of the *Scrapbook* tips have became outdated, simply not pertinent to the way we care for, handle and ride horses today. With that in mind, we've revamped the book a fifth time and titled it *Helpful Hints for Horsemen*, which was the subtitle on all the former books. It presents all new material published in *Western Horseman* in the last dozen or so years. But like its predecessors, it also contains some of Steffen's favorite ideas from the first four works. In fact, you'll find one "Vintage — Horseman's Scrapbook" tip in each of the 12 chapters.

Helpful Hints for Horsemen is unique in that it's something you, our readers, have asked for, but you've also contributed greatly to it. On its pages you'll find hundreds of time- and money-saving ideas, plus innovative horsemanship tips from readers such as yourself, as well as the magazine's staff members.

Horse people helping other horse people — that's what *Western Horseman* has always been about. Thumb through the pages and see if there isn't something that will make your horse life better today!

— *Kathy Swan*
BOOK EDITOR

CONTENTS

1 EQUINE HEALTH CARE

No-Chew Bandages

HAVE YOU EVER had to bandage your horse's leg and come back the next morning only to discover your horse has pulled off the leg wrap? Here's a tip, shown to me by John Spruell, D.V.M., of Laredo, Texas, to fix this problem.

Put some ordinary laundry detergent in a jar or container and begin adding a small amount of water until you have a soapy paste. Then apply the paste to the outside of the completed wrap — the entire bandaged area. Horses don't care for the taste of soap and will leave the bandage alone. An added benefit comes at laundry time. Your cloth wraps will have their own built-in soap supply.

— *Dale Fredricks*
Laredo, Texas

Face-Fly Mask

YOU CAN EASILY MAKE a simple mask to protect your horse from face flies using the leg of an old pair of jeans, or a piece of heavy cloth measuring about 18 to 20 inches.

Step l. Cut off the pant leg at the knee, slit it from top to bottom, and spread it flat.

Step 2. Cut a horizontal opening for the ears, and vertical strips for the fringe, as shown. If you use jeans, the hem provides the necessary weight at the end of the fringe; if you use lighter material, knotting the end of each fringe will accomplish the same purpose.

Step 3. Put on the mask, and tie the two end fringes under your horse's throat to secure it. Although this mask isn't very sturdy, it's safe because it can easily tear off should the horse get it caught on something.

— *Mary Anne Oldman*
Issaquah, Washington

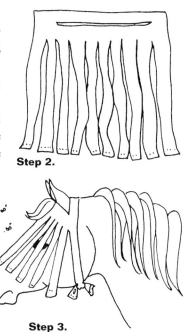

Step 2.

Step 3.

Palatable Medicating

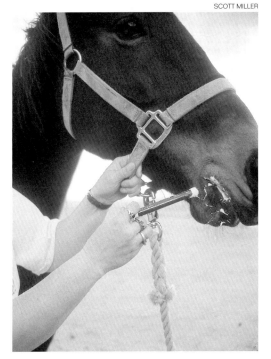

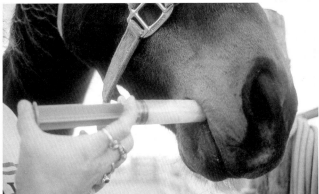

TO MAKE LIQUID medicine palatable to your horse, thus easier to administer, place a little frosting, molasses or applesauce in a syringe, as shown above. Then insert the medicine and another layer of the sweet treat.

To accustom your young horse to deworming, fill a clean, empty syringe with frosting, applesauce or molasses, as shown at left. Then squirt it into the corner of your youngster's mouth, as though you were deworming him. Repeat daily, until he accepts the syringe. When you actually deworm him it won't be a big deal.

— Jennifer Denison
Woodland Park, Colorado

Salt Trick

IF A HORSE won't drink strange water when away from home, ordinary table salt might do the trick. Just pour table salt into your hand, open the horse's mouth and put the salt on his tongue. You might have to repeat this once or twice, but it sure makes a horse start drinking.

— Pat Close
Elizabeth, Colorado

VINTAGE — Horseman's Scrapbook

Hock Socks

Here's a handy way to keep salve or other kinds of medicine on the hocks of a horse. A friend reports that it was nearly impossible to keep a bandage on the hocks of a mare that needed medicine applied daily to some wounds until he cut the tops off a pair of ribbed socks, cut a 2-inch slit in the center of each one to fit over the point of each hock, and slipped them into place. The socks really keep the salve on the wounds, and stay in place perfectly, he tells us.

— Randy Steffen

TOPS FROM
RIBBED SOCKS OR
← STOCKINGS

Foal Teething

SCOTT MILLER

SEVERAL YEARS AGO, I found two solutions to the problem of mares losing their manes and tails to teething foals.

The first solution I've used for about 8 years, but by combining it with the second, newer idea, I've virtually eliminated the problem.

The first solution is to combine ½-cup oil (corn or vegetable) with 2 tablespoons chili powder. Coat the mane and tail of the mare and other nearby horses liberally. When a foal starts chewing, usually at 2 to 3 weeks of age, he finds this distasteful. I call this taste imprinting, an addition to foal imprinting.

Tabasco sauce works equally well, but I've found other types of hot sauces don't last as long as Tabasco. Only one colt over the years actually liked the taste of Tabasco, hence his stable name of Mikie.

The next solution requires an old cotton lead rope, perhaps a broken one, about 12 inches long. I wrap the rope with synthetic sheepskin material and attach a snap on either end.

I attach the rope in the stall next to the creep feeder or the water bucket, or in the pasture or corral where the mares gather. I snap the rope to the fence horizontally, or use eye hooks on the wood inside the stall, about 3 feet from the ground. The foals chew and tug on the rope to satisfy their need to stimulate the gums. The sheepskin covering seems to work better than the plain cotton rope.

I've found this to be safe, provided the rope is placed high and is taut; that way, a foal can't get a leg through the loop or a jaw caught in it. Initially, I let the rope hang, but the foals seem more interested when it's attached horizontally. Usually the rope stays up for 6 to 8 months, and this technique seems to have no bad long-term effects.

Although a second application of sauce is sometimes needed on the mares' manes and tails, the sauce combined with the rope chew-toy has been successful for me.

— *Cheyanne West*
Ignacio, Colorado

Coat Cleaner

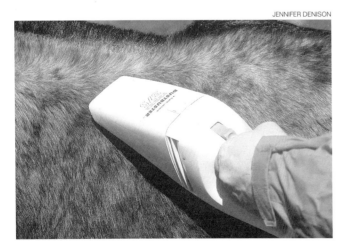

JENNIFER DENISON

EQUINE VACUUMS are wonderful for helping to keep a horse's coat clean, but they're expensive. Instead, buy a second-hand canister-style or hand-held vacuum. Either of these options works just as well as the expensive equine models.

— *Jennifer Denison*
Woodland Park, Colorado

Basting Brush

USE A basting brush to apply hoof dressing. Dip the brush in the dressing and brush it on your horse's hooves. To clean, slide the metal cap away from the bristles, soak the brush in dish detergent and water, then thoroughly rinse. Allow the brush to air-dry.

— *Jennifer Denison*
Woodland Park, Colorado

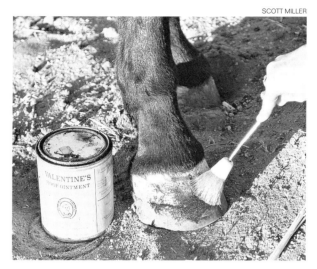

SCOTT MILLER

Glycerine Remedy

ON EXTENDED RIDES, or during long competitive events (like polo matches), a horse might get dry-mouthed. This can cause serious discomfort, especially given that he's carrying a bit in his mouth. I've found that squirting a small amount of glycerine into the horse's mouth will help keep it moist.

— *Pat Close*
Elizabeth, Colorado

First-Aid Kit Tip

SCOTT MILLER

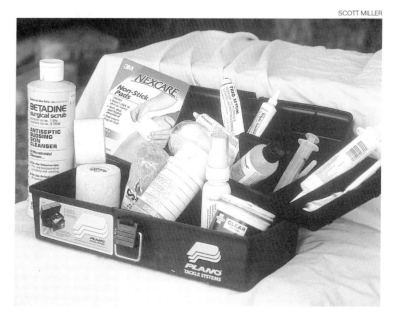

YOU SHOULD always carry an equine first-aid kit when traveling to shows and trail rides. It's aggravating, however, to search through rolls of tape and bandage material just to find your thermometer in the bottom of a box or bag. The best container I've found to store my first-aid supplies is a large fishing-tackle box with drawers. A two- or three-drawer tackle box provides lots of room in a handy carrying case, and numerous compartments help keep the items separate and easy to locate. You can store smaller supplies in the individual sections of the drawers, and place larger items in the bottom of the tackle box. I've used this first-aid kit for several years and have found it both sturdy and convenient.

— *Martha Branon Holden*
Yadkinville, North Carolina

Paste Worming

PASTE DEWORMERS are convenient to use, but occasionally a horse will spit out the paste if he has a wad of feed in his mouth. Even if he hasn't eaten for awhile, he can still have some feed lurking in his mouth.

To prevent this from happening, I first rinse the mouth with a garden hose, and tie up the horse for a few minutes. Then his mouth will be clean and dry when I insert the paste.

When doing this procedure alone follow these steps to make it easier. Hold the halter with four fingers of your left hand while putting your thumb gently into the horse's mouth, and pulling the lip toward your fingers. This gets the horse accustomed to something being in his mouth, and he'll be less likely to react when the tube is inserted.

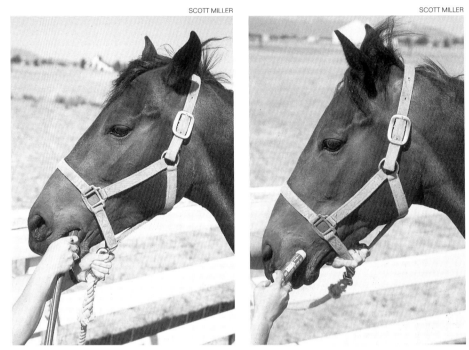

SCOTT MILLER   SCOTT MILLER

Dispense the dewormer evenly, and then hold the horse's head up so he swallows the paste instead of spitting it out.

— *Lynda Layne*
Winchester Bay, Oregon

Old Prescription Bottles

THE NEXT TIME you're cleaning out the medicine cabinet and have expired or finished prescriptions, save that old medicine bottle. Prescription bottles can be reused for a multitude of items.

Remove the old label, or cover it with masking tape if it won't come off, or attach a new label over the old one.

Sterile needles in various sizes, a few horse aspirins and matches wrapped in foil are just a few items that you can drop into each bottle and then place in a first-aid kit or saddlebags. Larger prescription bottles can hold syringes, little tubes of ointments, and such, and can also be stored on trailer-door compartments.

The bottle lids fit securely and, best of all, if broken, they're cheap to replace and you can recycle them by changing the labels.

— *Bonnie Davis*
Fremont, California

Wool Cooler

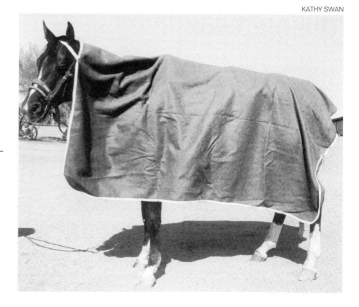

KATHY SWAN

No More Snowballs

JENNIFER DENISON

TO HELP PREVENT snow, ice and mud from balling up in the bottom of your horse's hooves, apply a thick coat of Pam nonstick cooking spray or petroleum jelly to his soles daily.

— *Jennifer Denison*
Woodland Park, Colorado

HERE'S A GOOD idea for all ropers. When I'm roping indoors in the winter, after I finish roping and my horse is hot and sweaty, I cover him with a 100-percent wool cooler. A horse cools out slower under a wool cooler. A cooler draws the heat from his body to the top of the cooler and keeps him from cooling down too fast and getting chilled. If he's an extra nervous and hot horse then I use two woolen coolers.

— *Wilbur Adank*
Hebron, Indiana

Foal Diaper-Rash Prevention

AS MANY horsemen know, foals about 7 to 10 days old usually develop diarrhea when their dams enter what's called their "foaling heat cycle." The liquid feces cakes the foal's buttocks, peels off the hair and looks like the mess it is.

Coating the buttocks with Vaseline prevents this from happening. If some manure has already caked on, wash it off with warm water, dry the area with a soft towel and then apply the Vaseline.

You can often minimize foal diarrhea by reducing the mare's grain ration a day or two before she enters her foal heat. Return to her regular ration after that heat cycle.

Caution: Foals dehydrate quickly, so if severe diarrhea persists, contact your veterinarian immediately.

— *Pat Close*
Elizabeth, Colorado

Pill Crusher

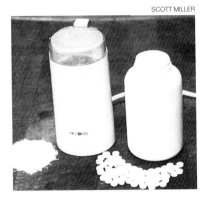

SCOTT MILLER

WHETHER YOU'RE doctoring a barnful, or just have a horse or two, this trick will come in handy. There are quite a few forms of medicine that come in tablets that require crushing before you administer them. If you count the number of tablets your horse needs and throw them in an electric coffee grinder, you can have them properly ground in a split second.

We even take it one step further for a couple of ranch horses that are on isoxsuprine. Instead of grinding their tablets everyday, we figure their dosage equals 2 tablespoons in powder form. Therefore, we simply grind an entire bottle and then return the powder to its original container. That way when those horses get their oats in the morning, we just add 2 tablespoons of isoxsuprine.

— Charlie Carrel
Sheridan, Wyoming

The Ice Trick

SCOTT MILLER

IF YOU have a horse that's a finicky drinker away from home, try adding ice cubes to his water.

Also, ice cubes may be used to help teach an orphan foal to drink milk. Simply put the milk replacer in a bowl, add some ice cubes and the foal invariably starts slurping it up.

— Pat Close
Elizabeth, Colorado

Coat Enhancer

JENNIFER DENISON

TO OFFER YOUR horse a little extra fat and to add shine to his haircoat, add ½ to 1 cup of corn oil to his grain daily.

— Jennifer Denison
Woodland Park, Colorado

Itch Soother

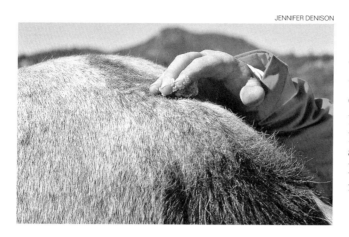

JENNIFER DENISON

HELP SOOTHE your horse's itchy skin with an oatmeal "mask." Add warm water to a packet of plain instant oatmeal, forming a thick paste. Apply the warm paste to the itchy area, and allow it to dry. Then rinse. Repeat daily as often as necessary.

— *Jennifer Denison*
Woodland Park, Colorado

Fetlock Sock

MY FILLY STEPPED on a nail that punctured a hole in the frog of her hoof. After treatment, she walked fairly well until she'd go outside. The hoof would get packed full of snow, putting pressure on the wound, and she'd start limping.

I came up with an idea that took care of this problem. I cut a piece of soft leather, which had fleece backing, from an old parka hood, and sewed it to the bottom of the foot of an old sock. I slipped the sock over the hoof and up the fetlock. The elastic held it in place, and my filly walked fine inside and out.

— *Gail Lotzer*
Sisseton, South Dakota

Tasty Treatments

STORE SNACK-size containers of applesauce in your equine first-aid kit. That way, if you need to give your horse medication, you can mix it with the applesauce, making it palatable for your horse. This is especially helpful when traveling with horses.

— *Jennifer Denison*
Woodland Park, Colorado

SCOTT MILLER

White Vinegar Fly Protection

SCOTT MILLER

WHITE VINEGAR is a wonderful cleaner, but it's also a useful fly repellent. To save dollars purchasing fly sprays during the summer, dilute three parts of your favorite fly spray with one part distilled white vinegar. Be sure to shake the bottle to recombine the mixture each time you use it.

— *Helena Hill*
Hart, Texas

Cribbing Cure

IN OUR BARN I've found an inexpensive way to stop horses from cribbing and windsucking. We have vertical bars on the front of each stall, and horses were chewing, or sucking wind, in the spaces between the bars.

To stop them, we took old horseshoes and placed them between the bars — one shoe between every two bars. It's also a good use for old horseshoes! If you don't have any, ask your shoer. He'll probably be glad to get rid of some. You can use staples to anchor the shoes in place.

BOARDS

Be sure to remove the nails before using the shoes, and secure the end of each shoe flush against the stall siding so nothing can get caught under it.

— *Marlene Partain*
Madison, Alabama

Medicated Grain

SCOTT MILLER

HERE'S HOW to get your horse to eat his grain when you must add medicine to it. The average horse won't eat it, because he either smells or tastes the medicine. But if you add molasses, about 2 generous tablespoons per gallon of grain, and stir thoroughly, this masks the odor and taste of the medicine. And because most horses have a sweet tooth, they'll readily eat the grain, medicine and all.

This also works well with daily deworming medicine, especially if you add molasses to the grain for one or two feedings beforehand. This accustoms the horse to the new sweet flavor, so that he's not the least bit suspicious when you add the deworming medicine.

— *Pat Close*
Elizabeth, Colorado

Fly Protection

HERE'S AN old-fashioned remedy I've used for over 50 years. First fry fatty bacon, and pour the grease into a plastic container, where it solidifies. Massage the grease around and over your horse's eyes and forehead. Flies disappear.

A horse sometimes gets hard to bridle because of sore, scabby ears due to flies. Massage a glob of bacon grease in each ear. Your horse will come to love it, and presto! Bridling is easy again.

Flies sometimes cause bald spots on the horse's head, but several rubbings with the grease will help the hair grow back.

This remedy is biodegradable, nontoxic to the horse and the environment, and cheap.

— *J.N. Swanson*
Carmel Valley, California

SADDLES

Stirrup Hobbles

Not using a stirrup hobble is a dangerous oversight, particularly on a child's saddle.

A properly adjusted stirrup hobble doesn't have to be removed to adjust stirrup length.

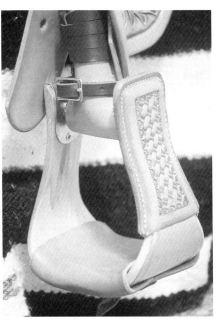

Postion the hobble buckle so that the tail of the strap points toward the horse.

MANY HORSE-RELATED ACCIDENTS cannot be prevented, but here's one simple thing you can do to help prevent hanging up and dragging if you fall from your horse. Saddlemaker Matt Plumlee, Eureka, Nev., has noticed over the years that most of the saddles people bring in to be cleaned or repaired are missing the stirrup hobbles, the small leather straps that buckle around the stirrup leathers just above the stirrups. He explains this is a very dangerous omission. As with almost all things related to horse gear, there's an important reason for these straps. The placement of the stirrup hobbles on the stirrup leathers prevents the stirrups from being loose and turning. If you were to fall and your stirrup turned, your foot is more likely to be caught; and if your horse were to spook, you could be dragged and injured badly or even killed.

Matt also says people mistakenly think that the stirrup hobbles need to be removed when they adjust the stirrup length. That's not true. After adjusting the length, pull the stirrup leathers from the top to make them lie flat again.

Another dangerous mistake is to leave the stirrup hobbles off on a child's saddle. It's doubly important for stirrup hobbles to be secured in case a short rider has to scramble for a foothold during a mount or dismount.

Correctly positioning the stirrup hobbles includes buckling them as tight and low as possible above the stirrups. Position the buckle on the side away from the leg, with the leather end of the strap that goes through the hobble buckle pointing toward the horse.

— Mike Laughlin
Eureka, Nevada

Different Way to Saddle

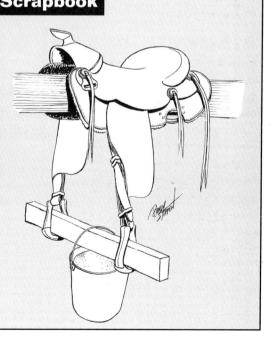

BILL SCRIVNER has not let age nor the lingering effects of a few horse wrecks stop him from riding.

However, Bill has an unusual method for saddling his horse. It's a method he's used for years as part of his training and handling program for young horses, and it's especially helpful now. It makes saddling easier for anyone who has trouble hefting a heavy western saddle aboard a horse.

Bill has rigged a rope and overhead pulley, which he uses to raise the saddle and then lower it onto the horse. Bill's an old cowboy (one of the last who did it the hard way) who appreciates all the new help available, while still holding onto all he's learned through the years from firsthand experience.

— *Ruth Scrivner*
Ivanhoe, Texas

VINTAGE — Horseman's Scrapbook

Stirrup Turner

A friend in Nevada writes that this is the way to really set the stirrups on a new saddle more quickly and positively than any other way he's heard of. He puts a double twist in the leathers after soaking them with a wet sponge. After running a 2-by-4 through the stirrups, he hangs a bucket of sand on the center of the board. This weight certainly should make the leathers hang straight and true.

— *Randy Steffen*

Rigging a Breast Collar

SOMETIMES A PHOTO in a ranch or training feature results in a few calls from our readers: "How did that guy have the breast collar rigged up on his saddle? It just doesn't look quite like mine does."

After checking the photos and questioning the callers further, it seems the major difference lies in how the breast collar is attached to the saddle, to ensure that it stays over the point of the horse's shoulder. Although most horsemen know that's where the breast collar should be positioned, attaching one so that it stays there isn't always easy. The breast collar often works down, right on the point of the horse's shoulder, where it rubs with every step he takes.

Sometimes this happens when the breast collar straps are run through the Ds, or cinch rings, on the saddle. The attachment can be so low that it allows the breast collar to drop, rather than holding it up and in the crease above the horse's shoulder. Some saddleries have addressed the problem by adding small dees above the cinch rings, toward the pommel, just for attaching the breast collar. However, depending on the saddle and the horse's conformation, the dees aren't always set high enough to keep a breast collar in place. If yours aren't, here are some photos with ideas that might help solve the problem.

Most any three-piece breast collar can be used in this "buckaroo style" if it is reasonably narrow, and 1½ inches is the average width used by buckaroos. Why? If the breast collar is too wide, more than 2 inches, the center ring isn't big enough to accommodate the body of the breast collar turning up, toward the saddle horn. That would require a bigger center ring.

— *Fran Devereux Smith*
Peyton, Colorado

Frequent *WH* contributor and clinician Buster McLaury has his breast collar rigged higher than most, but doing so ensures that the breast collar stays in place during a hard day of ranch work.

Clinician Marty Marten, author of the *WH* book *Problem-Solving*, uses D-rings to attach his breast collar, which is in good position here, well over the points of the horse's shoulders without being restrictive at the base of the horse's neck.

Marty's saddlemaker positioned small dees for the breast collar right at the pommel, higher than most would expect. The snap on the breast collar strap is a convenient idea.

No trip to the saddlemaker required for this set-up, where you can simply run the breast collar straps through the gullet and over the pommel.

Latigo Logic

MANY PEOPLE use nylon latigos because they're stout, serviceable and slick.

The slick part is good because it allows a person to cinch more easily than with some leather latigos, but it also has its downfall. The nylon latigo slides right out of the latigo carrier on your saddle. This can leave a person in a potentially dangerous situation with a dragging latigo.

The solution is to go back up and through the D-ring and to the latigo carrier. Go through the carrier twice to keep the latigo from sliding out. This ensures the latigo stays where it's supposed to be, not dragging under your horse.

— Don Straight
DeSoto, Iowa

Saddle Scabbard

MOST HORSEBACK hunters carry a rifle on the offside or right side. However, we prefer carrying the scabbard on the left side in a horizontal position. But there's one thing wrong with this: The scope rests on the scabbard. A lot of jolting around could easily knock the scope out of alignment.

We have eliminated this possibility with a special scabbard design. We designed the security strap to hold the rifle stock tightly, so the scope is

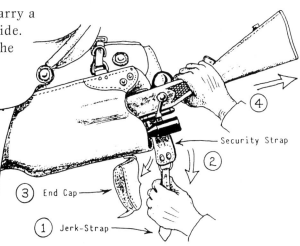

clear of the scabbard. The bolt is not exposed. We added the end cap to keep rain, snow and debris away from the scope. The jerk-strap allows quick release of the security strap, which you can fasten in several ways. For the snap end (with the jerk-strap), we use lift-the-dot snaps as they hold more securely.

You can quickly slip the rifle out of the scabbard, as shown in the sketch. When you're free of the stirrup, your left hand pulls down on the jerk-strap (1), which releases the security strap (2). At the same time, the end cap (3) falls down out of the way as you simultaneously withdraw the rifle (4). It all happens in one fluid motion. Your horse may continue to move, as is often the case when you're hurrying, and he'll actually pull the scabbard off the rifle, making withdrawal even faster.

— Al & Ann Stohlman
Ashcraft, British Columbia

Collar Tug Straps

BREAST-COLLAR TUG STRAPS can easily be replaced with stout 1-inch nylon dog collars. If you reverse the D-ring, as shown in the drawings, the collars have a built-in keeper to attach them to the main body of your breast collar.

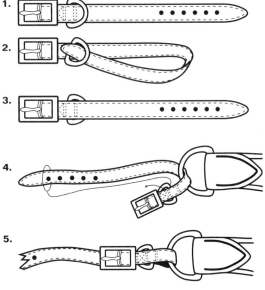

1. A 1-inch nylon-web dog collar. The D-ring is on the wrong side for our purposes.

2. Pull the end of the collar completely through the small D-ring.

3. Now the D-ring faces the other side of the collar.

4. Loop the collar through the breast collar D-ring as shown. Then pull the tail through the small D-ring on the dog collar.

5. Pull the dog collar snug. The small D-ring acts as a keeper, and your breast collar is ready to attach to your saddle.

— *Dale Fredricks*
Laredo, Texas

Slicker Trick

WHEN I PACKED and cowboyed many years ago, I tied my slicker behind the cantle with most of it hanging down. Brush, tree branches, or cactus often damaged it.

On the first of many pack trips into the Sierra Nevada range of California, I learned a new and very practical way to carry my slicker. I simply rolled it up, put it inside the denim leg cut off an old pair of blue jeans, and tied it behind the cantle. No more damaged slickers.

— *Dr. Robert M. Miller*
Thousand Oaks, California

Handy Spurs

DEPENDING ON which horse I'm using, I may or may not wear spurs. To keep spurs handy, I keep them on my saddle string. I run both buckles up a string, and buckle the lower one through a small hole punched near the top of the string.

When I need my spurs, they're right there, not buried in the tack room.

— *Jan Guelff*
Seeley Lake, Montana

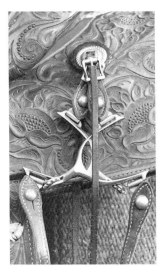

Broomstick Trick

TO TRAIN STIRRUPS TO LIE in the proper position, place the saddle on a rack or stand, twist a stirrup into the proper position, then twist it another half turn. Run a broomstick through the stirrup and under the saddle; then twist the other stirrup in a similar fashion and bring the stick on through. Just one or two overnight treatments will help the stirrup leathers and fenders assume the right shape. Dampening the leather also helps speed up the process.

Most new, top-quality saddles come with stirrups that are already properly positioned. But the broomstick trick works on any saddle that's bent out of shape.

— Marc Bonham
Cheyenne, Wyoming

Center-Fire Cinch

HORSES SOMETIMES develop a cinch sore, or a wound in the cinch area. Often the horse must be laid up until the injured area heals. But if your saddle is double-rigged, sometimes the horse can continue working if you adjust the cinch so it doesn't affect the area. I call this center-firing the cinch. Simply tie off the latigo to the rear-cinch dee.

If your cinch has single rigging, you can tie off the latigo to a rope run behind the cantle. It's more difficult to slide the latigo through the loop in the rope, so make sure you get the cinch snug enough.

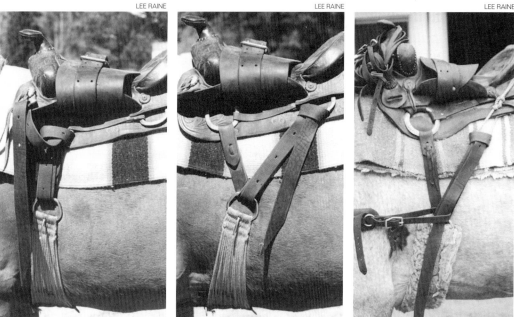

LEE RAINE   LEE RAINE   LEE RAINE

Normal position of the cinch. | Tying off the latigo to the rear dee on a double-rigged saddle. | Tying off the latigo on a single-rigged saddle.

— Mike Laughlin
Eureka, Nevada

Too-Long Leathers

GETTING A FOOT hung up in a stirrup is something all horsemen dread. On many saddles, the stirrup leather ends come down on the outside of the fold, instead of inside. This can be a hazard if the strap is so long that it extends down past the top of the stirrup. It should be folded under and held up by a stirrup hobble strap or it should be cut off above the top of the stirrup.

That extra strap can bind a foot in the stirrup, especially when mounting and dismounting.

— *Don Straight*
DeSoto, Iowa

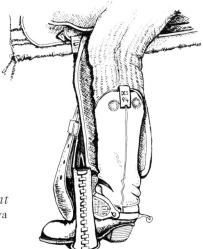

Lead-Rope Saddle Loop

MY DAD, John Christensen, showed me this fast and safe method of securing the lead when your horse is saddled.

Unbraid the saddle strings above the latigo carrier and place a ring between the strings and rebraid them. I use a 2-inch ring.

Fold the lead and push it through the ring to form the first loop. Fold the loose end of the lead again and push it through the first loop, which is snugged tight to hold the second loop.

To untie the lead, pull the loose end. This arrangement is pretty safe as the saddle strings generally break when a wreck occurs. You can easily attach the lead to the ring, even when you're mounted.

— *Jan Guelff*
Seeley Lake, Montana

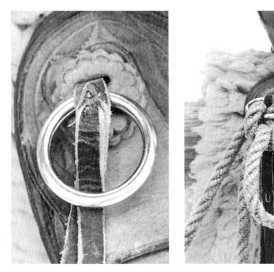

Latigo Longevity

MOST COW PUNCHERS keep their riggings well oiled, so the first place a latigo usually wears out is on the top end where the tail is always pulled tight.

You can avoid this by sewing a piece of latigo leather on the front of the rigging dee where your latigo pulls across. This reduces the wear and tear on the top end of the latigo, making it last a lot longer.

— *Buster McLaury*
Guthrie, Texas

Saddling Safety

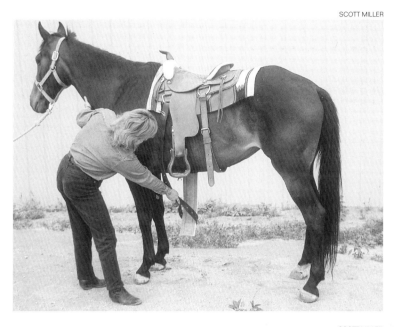

SCOTT MILLER

AT VARIOUS HORSE activities, I've noticed that quite a few horse people, kids in particular, reach way under the belly of a horse when saddling. Some of the youngsters, whose arms are too short to reach, squat down and get almost under the horse when reaching for the cinches.

This can be dangerous, even with a horse that has never offered to kick, and especially during fly season when horses stomp to shake off flies on their legs.

One way to make saddling safer, whether you're working with a seasoned mount or a green, skittish colt, is to use a couple of tricks practiced by range cowboys, who just naturally assume that any horse they walk up to is apt to be painted up for war.

When the saddle is in place and the cinches are hanging straight and unkinked on the off-side, make a loop in the end of your latigo. Stand close to the horse's shoulder and flip the loop under the belly and upward. You'll have to bend down to see what you're trying to catch, but you're less likely to get kicked. It'll take a few tries, but eventually you'll catch the cinch in the loop, and you can pull it under far enough to grab it.

For the back cinch, just stick your left leg under the belly till you can snag the cinch with your boot. If you're going to get kicked, it'll be in the boot or leg instead of the head.

— *Gary Vorhes*
Peyton, Colorado

SCOTT MILLER

Blevins Sleeve

HERE'S ONE WAY to keep from losing the sleeve on Blevins buckles. Rivet a light strap to the leather on the sleeve, then sew the other end to the stirrup leather. If the sleeve accidentally slides off, it's still attached and you won't lose it.

— *Art "Tango" Therriault*
Okmulgee, Oklahoma

Quick-Release Saddlebag Mounts

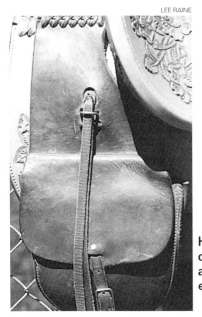

The leather concha with D-ring (left), which is attached as described below.

This is the pattern Mike uses to cut the hole and slit in his saddlebags.

Here's a pair of saddlebags attached the easy way.

A leather pattern piece is used to show how the saddle strings are pulled through the hole in the saddlebags, and the D-ring through the slit.

To fasten the quick-release saddlebag mount, pull the strings through the D-ring.

MIKE MEAUX, custom saddlemaker from Meeker, Colo., has devised mounts for saddlebags that make them quick and easy to remove from your saddle. No more untying bulky knots in your saddle strings.

Mike based his attaching devices on the way old cavalry saddles were rigged with permanent stand-up rings for attaching saddlebags. However, Mike makes a leather concha with a small D-ring riveted to it and then attaches the concha with the back saddle strings.

Mike puts two holes in the saddlebags—one round hole for the saddle strings to come through and one horizontal slit for the D-ring to come through. He then puts the saddlebags in place, runs the saddle strings through the round hole, the ring through the slit, and threads the saddle strings through the D-ring, which locks the saddlebags in place.

The strings remain neat and retain enough length to easily tie on a jacket or slicker. When you want to remove the bags, it's only a matter of a few seconds to pull the saddle strings out of the rings and pull off the saddlebags.

— *Mike Laughlin*
Eureka, Nevada

Dry Cleaning

WHEN YOU'RE cleaning a saddle, use an air pressure hose and blower attachment to remove dust and hair from tight crevices. It works great on a saddle and is terrific on the saddle lining, fluffing it as well as cleaning it. This also works on saddle blankets and pads.

Use compressed air from a tank or your own compressor by hooking a blower attachment to the air hose. The blow-gun also adapts to an air chuck used for filling tires. The compressed air comes out with enough force to blow the dirt away, and the gun makes it easy to direct the airstream into your saddle's nooks and crannies.

— *Lisa Jaquet*
Ellinger, Texas

Pinch Protection

WHENEVER YOUR HORSE has long hair, there's a chance of it catching in the cinch ring and latigo when saddling and unsaddling. This hurts him and pretty soon he'll be dancing around, maybe on your feet.

To protect him, get in the habit of sliding your left hand between the horse and the cinch ring. The motion holds everything out far enough to avoid catching hair.

— Don Straight
DeSoto, Iowa

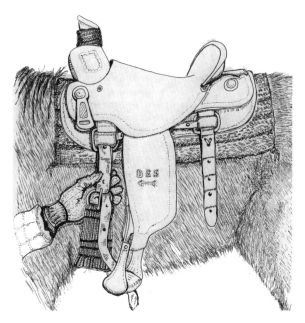

Saddle Britchin'

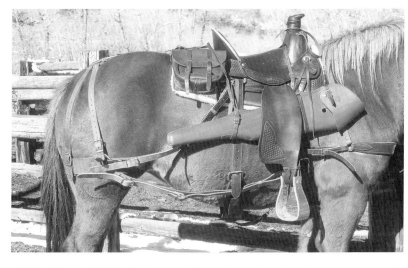

HUNTERS, COWBOYS and folks who ride their horses in rough country sometimes have a problem keeping the saddle in proper position on their horses. This can cause cinch and withers sores. One way to correct this problem is by using a "saddle britchin'," which works like a britchin' on a packsaddle. The straps around the horse's rear end keep the saddle from sliding forward the same way a breast collar keeps it from sliding backward. A ring needs to be added behind the cantle to attach the "spider" (the straps that go over the rump), and if your saddle is double-rigged, you can attach your quarter-straps (the side straps) to a D-ring on your back cinch.

Contact your local saddlemaker to have one made for you. A britchin' will make the mountains much easier on you and especially your horse.

— Mike Laughlin
Eureka, Nevada

Three-Slot All-Leather Rigging

THE THREE-SLOT RIGGING has become quite popular, especially in reining saddles. It seems, however, that a lot of people don't quite know what to do with it the first time they encounter a saddle rigged like this.

Here is the correct way to cinch a horse with this type of rigging.

— *Dale Fredricks*
Laredo, Texas

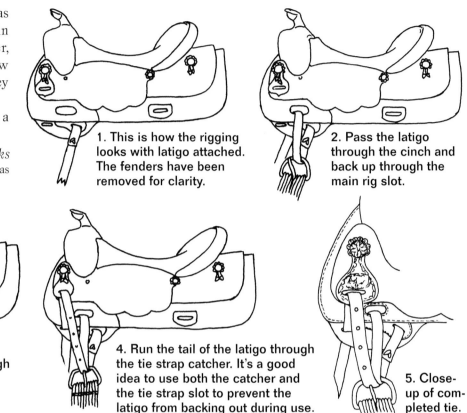

1. This is how the rigging looks with latigo attached. The fenders have been removed for clarity.

2. Pass the latigo through the cinch and back up through the main rig slot.

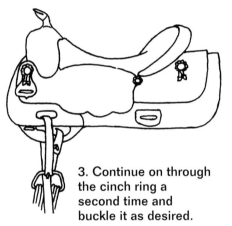

3. Continue on through the cinch ring a second time and buckle it as desired.

4. Run the tail of the latigo through the tie strap catcher. It's a good idea to use both the catcher and the tie strap slot to prevent the latigo from backing out during use.

5. Close-up of completed tie.

Snug Rope Strap

MATT PLUMLEE, saddlemaker and buckaroo from Eureka, Nev., snugs his rope to his saddle by taking two or three wraps around the rope counterclockwise with the rope strap. Then he makes one loop clockwise around the horn before buckling the strap.

This method keeps your rope from flopping around, and can also be handy to grab if the horse should blow up and buck.

To keep your rope ready for use, remember to coil the loop so that the honda is on the outside of the coil and pointing forward. This allows you to free your rope and build a loop quickly.

— *Mike Laughlin*
Eureka, Nevada

Stirrup Hoods

HOODS ON STIRRUPS are an added safety factor for young riders. Here's an easy way to construct and attach them so they can easily be removed when they're no longer needed.

Cut out a paper pattern to fit the stirrup measurements, and punch the holes where needed in the hood leather. Then, run leather thongs around the stirrup, through the hood, through the conchas and fasten them just like on chaps or saddle strings.

The hoods are simple to put on, and eliminate the danger of a small foot slipping through the stirrup and having a youngster get "hung up."

— *Dick Spencer*
Colorado Springs, Colorado

SLIT AND PULL THROUGH...

THEN SLIT THE OTHER ONE AND PULL THROUGH.

THONGS

HOOD   STIRRUP   CONCHAS

Handy Saddle Cover

DO YOU NEED a lightweight saddle cover to stow in your saddlebags for an unexpected rain shower? Or maybe you'd like an inexpensive dust cover for a saddle sitting on a rack at the barn. Here's a quick and fairly sturdy fix for either circumstance.

Many horsemen purchase bagged sawdust or shavings for use in the trailer, at a trail ride camp or during a show circuit. Keep the heavy-duty plastic bag to use as a saddle cover.

Lay a standard shavings bag flat on the floor, with one end open and the other end pleated and closed. Cut lengthwise up the center of the bag from the open end to, but not through, the pleats. Spread open, the bag makes a handy saddle cover.

Place the pleated end over the horn and pommel; the pleats help shape the bag to the front of the saddle. Then unfold the bag to drape it over the cantle and skirts. The shavings bag is plenty long to tuck under the rear skirts and wide enough to cover the entire saddle seat and about halfway down the fenders.

A couple of pluses: The shavings bag is heavier weight than most standard garbage sacks, which many of us carry for emergencies, and almost as easy to pack. Most horsemen already have shavings bags on hand.

— *Fran Devereux Smith*
Peyton, Colorado

BITS AND BRIDLES

Young Horses and Snaffle Bits

YOUNG HORSES have tender skin around the corners of their mouths that often gets bruised when a snaffle bit is introduced in the training process. This doesn't necessarily mean that the trainer or rider is heavy-handed; simply that the area around the mouth isn't used to accommodating iron or steel. Most young horses will show some pink from raw skin or even bleed slightly until they become accustomed to metal against skin.

To protect that area, put a little bit of ointment, such as aloe, lanolin or even petroleum jelly, around the corners of the mouth when the horse carries the bit. That keeps the area soft and pliable and prevents the bit from rubbing against the skin.

There are various horse products on the market specifically designed for wound treatment that work fine, but make sure the product is a mild one that doesn't contain harsh chemicals. Something that soothes while it heals is best.

— *Kathy Swan*
Scottsdale, Arizona

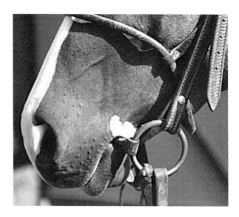

Broken-Rein Repair

I'M EMBARRASSED TO admit this has happened to me more than once.

I'm standing there, holding my horse by the reins, chatting with friends and not paying really close attention as my horse grabs a few bites of grass. Next thing I know, he's put a hoof on a rein, jerked up his head and broken the rein a few inches from the bit.

Usually, that little piece of rein hanging on the bit is too short to tie to, but don't throw it away. Try this method of joining the rein back together. Your rein will be a little shorter, but not much.

— *Kathy Doran*
Double Oak, Texas

Bosalitos

HERE ARE A COUPLE OF sketches of bosalitos (small bosals) you might want to keep for reference.

The back of the bosalito is tied in snug, up from the heel knot, with a little leather thong, which makes the snaffle bit much more effective.

With a mecate (pictured), there's just enough room left on the underside of the bosalito for the rope. Reins aren't shown in the sketch so you can see how everything is attached. The little latigo thong above the heel knot is used so the bosalito won't spread or break if the colt should pull back. You can also use a running martingale and a snaffle bit with the bosalito.

Here's another rig. The small mecate is clove-hitched just above the heel knot. This substitutes for a fiador, since the bosalito can't be pulled off if the horse jerks away. However, if he does set back when he is tied up, the clove hitch pulls so tight you'll have to cut it off. The knot used to tie the mecate around the horse's neck is the tried-and-true bowline, which won't slip and choke a horse.

— Dave Jones
Monticello, Florida

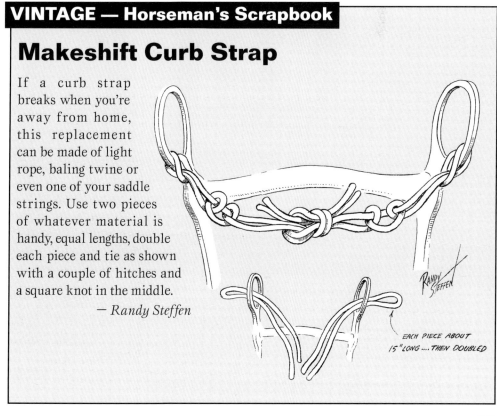

VINTAGE — Horseman's Scrapbook

Makeshift Curb Strap

If a curb strap breaks when you're away from home, this replacement can be made of light rope, baling twine or even one of your saddle strings. Use two pieces of whatever material is handy, equal lengths, double each piece and tie as shown with a couple of hitches and a square knot in the middle.

— Randy Steffen

EACH PIECE ABOUT 15" LONG ....THEN DOUBLED

Hackamore Driving Line

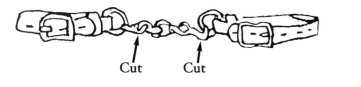

Cut   Cut

HERE'S MY INVENTION for driving a colt with a hackamore. First, find the type of curb chain that has leather loops for fasteners. Cut the chain, as shown, leaving the ring attached to each loop.

Buckle the loops to the bosal just above the mecate wraps. Then, snap a driving line to each ring. You're all set to drive a colt.

— *Sharon B. Morgan*
Dallas, Oregon

Attach Here

Driving Line

Chicago-Screws Trick

ON MANY BRIDLES, the loops for the bit are secured with Chicago screws. They're neat, especially on silver show bridles, but can be dangerous because the screws often work loose — resulting in the bit falling out of the horse's mouth.

Here's one way to solve the problem: Brush clear nail polish on the screw's threads, then quickly screw the two pieces together. This will keep them tight, but not so tight they can't be worked loose with pliers and screwdriver. This also works well on reins with snaps secured with the same type of screws.

— *Pat Close*
Elizabeth, Colorado

Browband Knot

FROM THE SHOW RING to the roping arena, the crisscross browband knot is popular. It's often seen with silver or horsehair ends, and it can really dress up your headstall. The knot is functional, too, because it makes your browband adjustable.

You can't use your existing browband because it won't be long enough. Instead, you'll need two pieces of leather attached to the long part of your headstall, with a slit cut in one of the pieces. Pass the end of the other piece through the slit, and loop each end over the back of the browband, tucking the ends through.

It's a good idea to leave the ends uncut until you have completed the knot. That way you can be sure they're even and the correct length.

— *Charlie Carrel*
Sheridan, Wyoming

War Bridle

I SAW A COUPLE of cowboys use this rig very effectively to lead horses through a sale ring.

Each cowboy had about 15 feet of old nylon lariat rope. As one cowboy eased up to the colt he wanted, he put the honda over the colt's neck. Then he'd grab it under the colt's neck, push the little loop through the honda and up over the nose.

To turn the colt loose, the cowboy pushed the nosepiece down and off the head. With a little tug on the rope, the whole thing came off and the horse was loose.

— Don Straight
DeSoto, Iowa

Throatlatch Keeper

HAVE YOU EVER WISHED there were a better way to keep the throatlatch of your bridle from falling out or being all on one side when you bridle your horse?

Use a small horseshoe-shaped piece of wire or small staple as a stop for the throatlatch. Simply press or tap the wire firmly into the left side leather of the throatlatch. Make sure it's in the correct spot to keep the brow band square on the horse's face and resting comfortably in front of the ears and to allow the throatlatch to fasten in the proper position. The throatlatch can't pull up through the brow band and be lop-sided or worse — lost. The throatlatch stays in the right position every time without readjustment. This comes in handy if you're riding a series of different horses with the same headstall.

— Mike Laughlin
Eureka, Nevada

Rein Leather for a Mona Lisa Bit

I COULDN'T FIND rein leathers to fit a small-ring Mona Lisa bit, so I designed a pair that turned out nicely. I used a new pair of stirrup hobbles, which were better sized for the bit's small rings. Although my hobbles had a larger, oval-shaped center, which I used to showcase a silver concha, the idea will work using straight-cut stirrup hobbles.

First, I punched an additional hole at the very end of the tab end of each hobble. Then I cut the buckle off the other end and punched two holes there to match the last two holes on the tab end. I also punched two matching holes on the oval face in the center of each hobble.

I put one end of the hobble around the bit ring, with the center oval to the outside. After aligning the two holes at each end of the hobble with those on the oval, I ran a leather tie string through them, lacing through the holes from the back to the oval face. I then added a leather concha with a silver concha on top before tying off the lacing.

In the other end-loop of the hobble, I fastened my mecate reins. I threaded each rein into the loop from the top, then wrapped it around so the tail hung down.

— Jo Schaaf
Atkinson, Nebraska

Recycled Bits

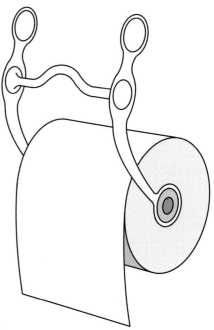

CURB BITS THAT ARE no longer in use can be made into rustic toilet-paper holders by adding a spring-loaded rod between the bit shanks. You can purchase an inexpensive tension rod for holding the paper at a local department store. The rein rings in the bit are too large to seat the ends of the rod, so glue two large washers inside the rings. The ends of the rod now fit snugly between the shanks.

The other end of the bit, where it's mounted to the wall, should hang freely. Two large staples are a good choice for mounting the bit on a solid wood wall. Or an old piece of barn wood makes a nice mounting board that can then be attached to any type surface. First, staple the headstall rings of the bit to the barn wood, then attach the wood base to the wall.

— Gary Kirchmeier
Cave Creek, Arizona

Halter/Hackamore Bit

I'D NEVER SEEN ONE of these outfits until I fixed one for myself — a nylon halter used in combination with a mechanical hackamore. This is what I use when I trail ride. I used to put the headstall over the halter, but I combined the two. It minimizes the headgear on the horse. I can ride with it and then tie up when I dismount.

I use two small nylon straps (about the size of a man's watchband) for attaching the hackamore bit to the rings in the halter. Draw the straps up snug so the mechanical hackamore is positioned properly on the nose. Then to prevent the nosepiece of the hackamore from dropping, I use a third strap to secure it to the nosepiece of the halter.

I keep the lead rope attached to the halter; and when I ride, I loop the end over the saddle horn.

— Mike Boren
Konawa, Oklahoma

Hackamore Helper

BY NECESSITY, THE HEADSTALL on a mechanical hackamore runs very close to a horse's eyes. This can be not only annoying to the horse, but also pose a risk of eye injury.

A simple and effective way to eliminate this problem is to put a strap on the headstall, midway between the adjustment buckle and the bit. Adjust the strap so that it runs just under the jaw of the horse. This pulls the buckle back and away from the horse's eye.

An old leather curb strap, if long enough, often works well for this.

STRAP

— Don Straight
DeSoto, Iowa

Short Chicago Screws

CHICAGO SCREWS commonly secure the bit to the bridle. Some horsemen don't like the screws, but I do, and I've never had any trouble with them. I do check them before I bridle a horse to make sure the screws are snug.

The screw used to be made as long as the receptacle. Recently, however, some Chicago  screws are being sold with a very short screw that barely seats in the receptacle. If such a screw loosens, it easily comes out of the receptacle. If you buy any tack with Chicago screws, unscrew them to check their length.

— Robert M. Miller, D.V.M.
Thousand Oaks, California

GEAR

Protective Leg Gear Storage

A MAJOR RULE of training is that the horse shouldn't be hurt, so we all should utilize some type of leg protection on our horses. That's easy enough because most brands of protective leg gear now fasten with Velcro®-type closures.

Through the years I've stored protective leg gear in milk cartons, laundry bags and on tack-room shelves. However, my means of storage caused problems, particularly with drying out the gear after I'd used or washed it. And I got lazy, not wanting to look for the left or right boot or front or back sizes I needed, and I worried about other animals carrying a boot away from the barn. The bottom line: I wouldn't utilize this valuable equipment as I should.

Then I came up with an idea that protected my leg gear and kept the front boots up front, the rear ones to the rear, left boots on the left, and right ones on the right. As a result, I've gone from using protective leg gear on my horse about 50 percent of the time to 100-percent usage.

I purchased some Velcro Sticky Back Strips, which you can find at most discount stores or any sewing shop. Then I cut the 4-by-2-inch strips into 1-by-2-inch pieces. Next, I stapled the strips to the walls of my barn because the sticky back didn't stick to wood very well.

Now after each use I can easily hang my protective leg gear on the Velcro patch. Because the boots are open to air, they dry better. Animals can't carry off the gear, and I can easily reach for the gear appropriate for the horse's leg I want to protect. My equipment stays clean and in good repair. The Velcro patches also work on the tack door of your trailer.

— *Jimmy Driver*
Certified Driver; Lebanon, Tennessee

The Old Sleeping Bag

DON'T THROW AWAY your old sleeping bag! It makes a perfect winter blanket for your horse. Cut two slots at the base of the neck, two slots right behind the front legs and two slots by the withers. Put straps through the slots to tie on the blanket. For a cheap tie use baling twine. For a different look use brass eyelets in place of the cut slots. For a more snug fit use light bungee cords. A bonus: Most sleeping bags are water repellent.

— *Joe Feist*
Ballantine, Montana

Frozen Snaps

FROZEN SNAPS can be troublesome during the winter. Solve the problem with a tube of the deicer that's used on car-door locks or a can of spray deicer for windshields. It works on any snap.

— *Wilbur W. Adank*
Hebron, Indiana

Snug Wraps

I WAS RIDING a barrel horse and had wrapped his back legs with conventional leg wraps. Even though I took great measures to ensure they'd stay snug, I didn't want to risk the wraps coming undone and causing an accident. I purchased an inexpensive pair of knee-high stockings, tore the foot open at the seam and pulled the stocking over the hoof and up toward the hock.

The elastic at the tip of the stocking fit right over the top of the wrap perfectly, and was neither too tight nor too loose. The wraps held very nicely and were in good enough shape to be used again, if needed.

— *Marilyn Grantier*
Texarkana, Texas

VINTAGE — Horseman's Scrapbook

Saddle-Pad Holder

This tip is from a reader in Kansas. He punches a hole in the front of his saddle blanket, threads a piece of leather string through it, and ties it so the loop formed is long enough to hook over the saddle horn when the blanket and saddle are in place on the horse's back. He says this sure keeps the blanket from sliding off in rough country, especially on a high-withered pony that you don't have to cinch up tight to keep your saddle in place.

— *Randy Steffen*

Ear Protector

HERE'S A SIMPLE, inexpensive and safe way to keep flies from irritating your horse's ears — protect his ears with pantyhose. We've used this easy-to-make protector on our horses' ears for several years, and most horses tolerate the headgear. Plus, if the pantyhose get caught on anything, they rip or pull right off the horse's head. You can even use this under a bridle when you're riding into a fly problem.

It takes only about five minutes to make an ear protector from a pair of pantyhose — new or used. If used, runs in the lower leg are no problem because that portion is cut off to make the ties. But don't use hose with runs in the thigh area because that's what goes over the ears, and flies can still get to your horse's ears through the runs.

Lay the pantyhose flat on the floor and cut off each leg somewhere between thigh and knee. You want at least 6 or 7 inches from the crotch down the leg to cover the ear and allow for a knot in the end. Save the cut portions to use later.

Next, cut the center front and center back hose seams down to the crotch lining. Hose with a triangular lining there fit well between the horse's ears. If there's no lining area, leave about 5 inches intact through the crotch,

to cover the horse's poll, when you cut the center seams.

Now tie the cut leg portions of the hose, toe hanging free, to either side of the waistband so you can fasten the ear protector around your horse's throatlatch. But, before you tie on the protector, be sure the horse's ears are clean so you don't trap any buzzing flies inside the hose.

Gently pull the short, knotted thigh pieces over each ear so the crotch area rests between the horse's ears and the ties are hanging loose on either side of his head. Then tie the hose under the throatlatch in a snug bow. The stretchiness of the pantyhose allows for a comfortable fit, and the hose should rip or slide right off your horse's head should the ear protector get caught on anything.

— *Terri Ann Wear*
Boise, Idaho

Lead-Rope Repair

I HAD A handful of old lead ropes hanging in the tack room. All were good heavy ropes, but the snaps were no longer functional. I cut off the old snaps and put new ones in place using rope clamps from the local hardware store. Unfortunately, these lasted a very short time. No matter how tight I squeezed them down on the rope, the clamps wouldn't stand up to an 1,100-pound colt.

The solution was fairly simple. I replaced the rope clamps with a heavy link of chain. The illustration shows a knot at the end of the rope, but I made a number of these and just melted the end of the nylon lead and whacked the chain link a couple of times with a hammer. If the snap breaks again, it'll be easy to fix.

— *Don Straight*
DeSoto, Iowa

Egg-Crate Foam Saddle Pads

I'VE ALWAYS felt that using natural animal-hair pads (real sheepskin, woven wool or hair felt) causes fewer sore backs on horses than using most synthetic materials.

However, I found an exception on the Ulupalakua Ranch on the Hawaiian island of Maui. This hard-riding outfit runs 5,000 head of cattle and 150 elk on 25,000 acres of steep pasture on the slopes of Mount Haleakala, the island's 10,000-plus-foot volcano. This ranch has virtually eliminated their sore-back problems by using egg-crate foam saddle pads. Place the pads crate-side down on the back, and cover them with a regular pad before you put the saddle on the horse's back. Despite the warm tropical climate, the humidity and the steep terrain, back problems are no longer a factor for ranch horses.

Ranch manager Ed Rice said the egg-crate pads are made by Keyston Brothers, based in Nevada. You can order the pads through your local tack store.

— Robert M. Miller, D.V.M.
Thousand Oaks, California

Spur Stabilizers

TO PREVENT your spurs from riding up your boots, secure them with a loop of inner tube. Using a knife or scissors, cut a 2-inch-thick section of inner tube. Place the loop around the neck of your spurs, then stretch it over your boot heels.

— Jennifer Denison
Woodland Park, Colorado

Blanket Clamps

WAYNE RICHARDS of Kansas City, Kan., has ridden the trails at Golden Hills Trail Ride in Raymondville, Mo., every year since the outfit opened for business. While visiting the campgrounds, I saw Wayne's blankets hanging on his trailer; he said it's the best way he's found to deal with wet saddle blankets when he's camping with his horses.

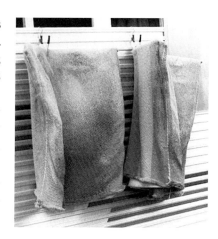

No major work is required, just a simple trip to a hardware store. Wayne purchased alligator clamps, which have a hole in the handle, and an S-hook for each clamp. He hangs a hook over a slat in the trailer, then threads the bottom end of the S through the handle of the clamp.

Often people throw damp saddle blankets over a slat on the trailer or across an inside divider, but often the blanket is knocked off and picks up hay, burs and such. That won't happen when the blanket is clamped to the side of the trailer, and it's also a great way to air out wet, smelly blankets.

— Fran Devereux Smith
Peyton, Colorado

Saddle-Pad Power Wash

IMITATION FLEECE saddle pads are popular because they're soft and easy on a horse's back, as well as easy to wash and keep clean.

Unfortunately, they're a little awkward to wash in a washing machine, especially when they've been used during the winter or spring when a horse is shedding, or when he's hard to perfectly clean before a ride. When the pad is full of hair, dirt and sweat, you might take a dim view of having it in your washing machine.

An easy way to clean those dirty pads is with a power washer. The force of the spray lifts out the dirt and hair nicely. You don't need soap, just waterpower. Soap residues in a pad can irritate a horse's back. The power washer can get pads cleaner than a washing machine, and you don't have all that mess and hair left in the washing machine.

— *Heather Smith Thomas*
Salmon, Idaho

Breakaway Honda

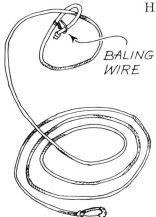

BALING WIRE

HERE'S AN easy way to fix a breakaway honda for breakaway roping practice.

First, unthread the rope out of the regular honda, so there's no loop in that end to trap the roper as he ropes with a breakaway loop in the other end. Wind a piece of baling wire about 8 inches from the knot in the tail of the rope and twist it tight with pliers.

Leave one length of wire protruding from the twist. Wind this around the rope just in front of the knot, and pull tight enough to hold the honda in place for roping, but not so tight that it won't pull loose easily when the roped animal puts pressure on it.

— *Chuck King*
Colorado Springs, Colorado

Snug Fit

LEATHER ON spur bands makes the spurs fit snugly on the boot counters. Leather against leather doesn't slip nearly as much as a regular steel band against boot leather.

Place a thinned-down piece of latigo leather around the heel band and hand-sew it along the bottom of the band to hold it in place. Cut slots in the leather to free the swinging spur buttons. Make slits in the leather on the outside of each band, and run a tie-down strap through the slits. With the tie-down strap in front of the boot heel and buckled tight, the spurs stay in place.

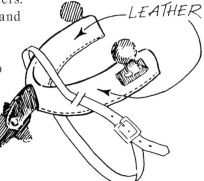

LEATHER

— *Chuck King*
Colorado Springs, Colorado

How Many Wraps Can a Rope Strap Hack

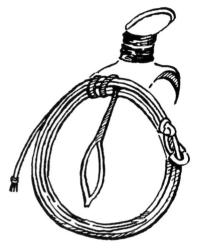

THIS TIP shows how to carry a catch-rope so it won't be lost if the horn-slot slips off the saddle horn. When attaching the rope to the saddle fork, take the first two wraps of the strap around all the coils of ropes. Then, take the third wrap around only two coils of rope before you slip the slotted end over the saddle horn.

Should the slot come loose from the horn, the rope strap will bind where it goes around the two coils, and the rope won't be lost. In other words, a wrap of this kind won't unwind, because a carefully wrapped rope strap traps a rope every time. Using the strap in this manner also tends to keep the coils from slipping back and forth.

— Chuck King
Colorado Springs, Colorado

Blanket Straps

THE FASTENERS used on the belly straps of many horse blankets and sheets often come loose, especially when a horse is turned out. To ensure this doesn't happen, use a twist tie. After inserting it as shown, twist it tight. These ties often come on loaves of bread and on other plastic bags, such as those used for veggies in supermarkets.

— Pat Close
Elizabeth, Colorado

Steer-Tie String

METHODS OF carrying a steer tie string vary in different areas of cattle country. Usually the tie is hung from the chaps belt or the saddle. Another method is to carry it around the horse's neck.

The string is about 12 feet long, and has a knot at each end and no honda. When a steer is finally roped out in the pasture, take two half hitches around his horns with the tie string. Tie off the hitches in a manner that prevents them from pulling too tightly around the horns. Then use the rest of the string to tie the steer to a tree until the rider has time to lead him into the corrals. The sketch shows the knot that holds the string around the horse's neck.

— Chuck King
Colorado Springs, Colorado

Blanket Measurement

PUZZLED BY what size blanket or sheet to buy for your horse? Lots of folks are when they sort through a stack of blankets or read in a catalog that blankets are available in "sizes 66-82."

"If you're buying a blanket off the shelf, you need only one measurement on your horse," explains Maggie Clark. "That's the length of chest to the edge of his tail. Then I always add another inch or two to make sure the blanket is roomy. Say the horse measures 78 inches; I'd buy him a size 79, or an 80 if you use a sheet or liner under the blanket."

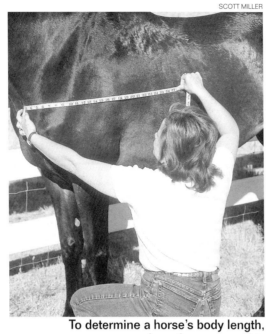

To determine a horse's body length, measure from the center of his chest, back to the edge of his tail.

Maggie owns and operates C Bar M Enterprises, located near Colorado Springs, Colo., which specializes in producing custom blankets renowned for their fit and warmth. To ensure that a blanket fits properly and stays in position, Maggie always takes two more measurements: body depth and neck opening (see photos).

She points out that the body depth, or heart girth, measurement is especially important because some blankets are too shallow. "That exposes too much of the belly to cold air, and the horse grows long hair. You can use a 'belly warmer' with the blanket, but it isn't necessary if the blanket is deep enough in the first place. Then it'll trap more body heat."

A poorly fitted neck opening is another problem. "If the opening is too low, the blanket chafes the points of the shoulders, rubbing off the hair. This happens a lot with high-necked horses, such as Saddlebreds, some Arabs, and even some modern Quarter Horses."

Proper fit is also determined by conformational features. Says Maggie, "The average Thoroughbred has more prominent withers and shoulder points than other horses, and so his blanket must be cut accordingly. Horses with a low necks, steep croups, or swaybacks also need special adjustments. A blanket for a horse with a normal back usually has a 3-inch drop, but a swayback horse requires a deeper drop."

Some horse owners don't like a blanket to cover the withers, fearing that the blanket will rub the withers and make them sore. But Maggie says this won't happen if the blanket fits properly. Her blankets

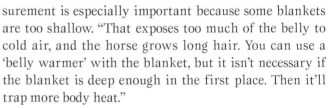

When the neck opening is too low, as shown here, it chafes the horse's shoulders.

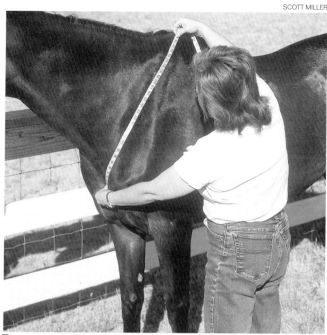

To measure the neck opening, stretch the tape from the base of the neck to just in front of the withers.

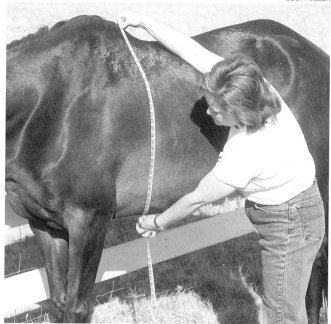

For body depth, measure from the highest point of the withers to the bottom of the barrel, just behind the front legs.

have satin lining at the withers for extra protection.

She adds, "Sometimes a blanket that's cut back so the withers aren't covered can still sore the withers where they tie into the back if the blanket fits too tightly in this area."

A too-small blanket can cause problems, too. "Some people figure that if the blanket covers the body, it fits okay; but it can actually be too small. This frequently happens when a person buys a blanket for a young horse; as the horse grows, the owner loosens the front opening to allow the blanket to slip back and cover more of the body. Eventually the blanket will 'bind' the horse in the withers, making it sore and also rubbing hair off the points of the shoulders," Maggie explains.

Maggie uses either a butt strap, or leg straps, whichever the customer prefers. Both keep a blanket from blowing in the wind, and leg straps have the added advantage of helping prevent the Houdini-types from wriggling out of their blankets. One disadvantage of a butt strap: It can be soiled by urine and manure.

How heavy a blanket does your horse need? According to Maggie, "It depends on his blood count, barn temperature, whether he's stalled all the time or turned out during the day and if you're trying to keep a show coat on him. Sometimes you can get by with a lighter blanket for mild winter weather, and then add a sheet or blanket-liner underneath for colder weather."

— Pat Close
Elizabeth, Colorado

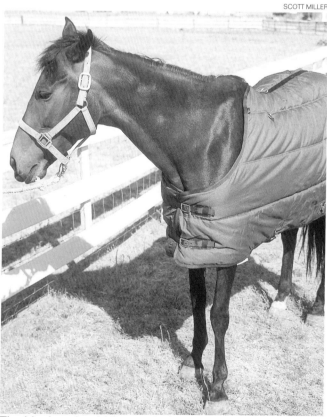

The blanket should fit snugly, but comfortably, in front. This blanket, not custom-made for this horse, is too low across his chest, Maggie says. Ideally, it should be about 1½ inches higher.

KNOTS

Halter-Puller Knot

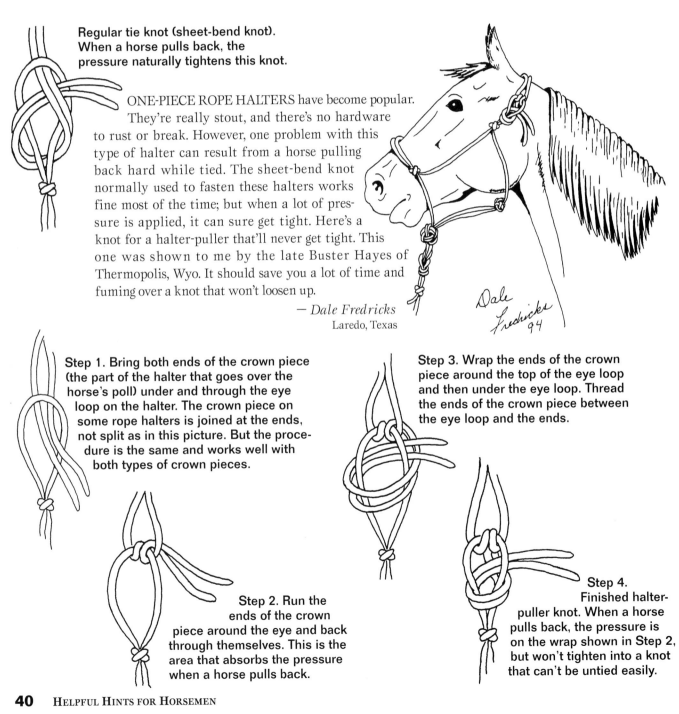

Regular tie knot (sheet-bend knot). When a horse pulls back, the pressure naturally tightens this knot.

ONE-PIECE ROPE HALTERS have become popular. They're really stout, and there's no hardware to rust or break. However, one problem with this type of halter can result from a horse pulling back hard while tied. The sheet-bend knot normally used to fasten these halters works fine most of the time; but when a lot of pressure is applied, it can sure get tight. Here's a knot for a halter-puller that'll never get tight. This one was shown to me by the late Buster Hayes of Thermopolis, Wyo. It should save you a lot of time and fuming over a knot that won't loosen up.

— *Dale Fredricks*
Laredo, Texas

Step 1. Bring both ends of the crown piece (the part of the halter that goes over the horse's poll) under and through the eye loop on the halter. The crown piece on some rope halters is joined at the ends, not split as in this picture. But the procedure is the same and works well with both types of crown pieces.

Step 2. Run the ends of the crown piece around the eye and back through themselves. This is the area that absorbs the pressure when a horse pulls back.

Step 3. Wrap the ends of the crown piece around the top of the eye loop and then under the eye loop. Thread the ends of the crown piece between the eye loop and the ends.

Step 4. Finished halter-puller knot. When a horse pulls back, the pressure is on the wrap shown in Step 2, but won't tighten into a knot that can't be untied easily.

Tree-Tie

ASK DORIS SHARP of California what she likes best about tying her horses to shade trees in front of her barn and she'll tell you, "The patience it develops. Also the absence of broken lead ropes."

In the shade of a large tree, three or four horses can be tied at one time. Doris says they have more freedom when tied overhead, giving them a less confined feeling. And there's no way a clever horse can untie himself, or chew on the rope.

Doris permanently tied several lead ropes to stout overhead limbs. Then it's easy to lead a horse over and snap him on.

Tying outside also has other advantages. If a horse is confined to his stall most of the time, tying him outside breaks the monotony as he watches what's going on around the barn. And in the summer, sometimes it's cooler under a tree than inside the barn. It's also a handy place to put a horse while his stall is being cleaned or while he's drying after a bath. And for a halter horse that must have a neck sweat on after a workout, there's no way he can rub it off while tied overhead to a tree limb.

— Lynda Layne
Winchester Bay, Oregon

VINTAGE — Horseman's Scrapbook

Grazing Rope

For those horsemen who like to let a horse or pony graze at the end of a rope while they're doing a little relaxing, too, here's a way to keep the lead rope from getting snarled up in the horse's feet. Tie a scrap piece of rope as shown, securing it to the horse's mane to keep it from slipping out of place; then run the lead rope between the horse and the rope, and you'll have it made. This is not to be used for staking a horse — only when the end of the rope is being held by someone.

— Randy Steffen

Makeshift Halter

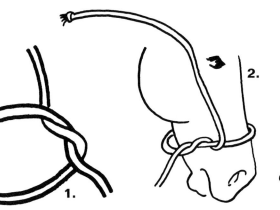

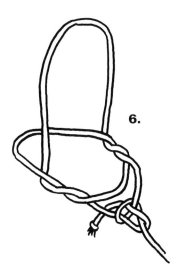

OSCAR MARSH of the Wooden Shoe Ranch in Laramie, Wyo. learned to tie this halter from his father. It was used on broncs; when tied correctly, it stays in place real well. To tie it:

1. Put an overhand knot loosely near one end of the rope.
2. Slip the loop formed by the knot around the horse's nose. The overhand knot is on the right side of the horse's nose.
3. Take one end of the rope over the horse's poll, just behind the ears. Bring the rope down the left side of the horse's head and take it under, then over and under the nose loop.
4. Using a bowline knot, tie the end of rope that was taken over the horse's head to the lead-shank part of the rope to complete the halter.

I use a bowline. Oscar often used the horse's mane tied in a knot (5) to hold the halter in place on top of the horse's neck. The complete halter is shown in drawing No. 6.

— Chuck King
Colorado Springs, Colorado

Quick Release

IF YOU TIE ON hard and fast when roping cattle, and use an aluminum or plastic horn knot, here's a quick-release system that works well. Drill a ¼-inch hole in your horn knot and tie on a 10-inch leather thong.

If you get into trouble and need to get your rope loose fast, grab the leather and pull it toward your left knee, or where it would be if you were off your horse. One try and you'll see how much faster this is, and it could sure save you some trouble.

— Wilbur Adank
Hebron, Indiana

Figure-Eight Horn Knot

DOCTORING that old bull for hoof rot in the middle of a sagebrush flat can sometimes get a little western. When only two cowboys are present, one has to do the veterinary work while the other holds the heels. Old Bay has to take care of the head rope. Well, as usual, you left you horn loop on the dash of your pickup. I'm a firm believer in the figure-eight horn knot and have used it many times in this situation. Some people might think it would pull off, but I've seen guys rope hundreds of big cattle with this and it's never failed yet. The safety part of this is that if you get in a tight spot, just push on the tail of the rope (B) and it loosens right up. The arrow on (A) shows the part that goes over the horn.

A safety reminder: Don't tie on hard and fast if you or your horse are inexperienced ropers.

— *Don Straight*
DeSota, Iowa

Cinch Trick

ARE YOU TIRED of your horses breaking halters when they pull back? Here's a way to prevent that.

You'll need a strong nylon rope and a cotton or mohair string cinch with rings that don't have tongues in them. If there's a tongue, remove it with a pair of stout pliers or bolt cutters. Place the cinch over the horse's neck, just behind his poll, with the rings underneath his neck. Slide the tie rope under the halter and below the jaw of the horse, and tie a bowline. Tie the horse to a solid object that won't break if he pulls back. Whenever the horse pulls back, the cinch takes the pressure, but doesn't hurt the horse.

This trick will help in three ways: 1. You won't break any more halters. 2. The horse will learn he can't break lose when he pulls back. 3. You'll remove the pain associated with pulling back. Pain causes fear, and fear is the main factor that causes a horse to pull back.

— *Mike Kevil*
Cave Creek, Arizona
www.startingcolts.com

43

Packsaddle Latigo Safety Knot

1. From the left, bring the point of the latigo under the ring in the packsaddle rigging.

2. Pull the latigo under the rigging ring, above the wraps taken to secure the cinch, to form a loop on the left side.

ART HEDIN, Kalispell, Mont., a long-time packer in the Bob Marshall Wilderness area, says that when packing horses and mules, it's a good idea to have a quick-release knot on the packsaddle latigos. That way, if a wreck occurs and a packsaddle turns, you can quickly pull the loose end of the latigo, loosen the cinches, and release the packsaddle before the equipment and pack animal get hurt. Here's a knot that is flatter and less bulky under the packs, which helps eliminate galling the pack animal.

— *Mike Laughlin*
Eureka, Nevada

3. Then pull the loop tight. The rigging ring acts as a lock on the loop.

4. Another loop of latigo may be inserted through the first loop and tightened down if you have a great deal of excess latigo. One loop is enough to secure the latigo.

5. Here's how the knots securing two packsaddle cinches look when complete.

6. To release the knot, simply jerk the tail.

Breakaway Hitch

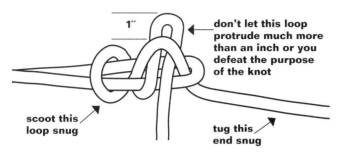

1″

don't let this loop protrude much more than an inch or you defeat the purpose of the knot

scoot this loop snug

tug this end snug

IN GRATITUDE to the older, more experienced folks who have saved my bacon on occasion, I offer this hitch for tying one pack animal to the one ahead.

As a packer who has averted more than my share of potential catastrophes by using proper knots, I believe the hitch shown is superior because one smart tug and the horse or mule is free, instantly, even if he's been hanging back on the rope all day long.

— *Jed Greene*
Yreka, California

Bowline Catch Rope

THE BOWLINE, a knot that doesn't slip, can be tied in various ways. The accompanying sketches show how Bob Scott of Scottsdale, Ariz., ties the bowline around a horse's neck. This method is fast, because a portion of the knot is tied in the rope before the horse is approached. When the horse is reached, the bowline is tied by simply placing one end of the rope through a loop in the pretied portion of the knot and pulling on the other end of the rope.

Figure 1 shows how the knot is started with a coil at one end of the rope. The end hanging down to the right will eventually go around the horse's neck. Figure 2 shows how the rope in the back part of the coil is brought over the rope in the front part of the coil and shoved through the coil to form the slip knot shown in Figure 3.

With this pretied portion of the knot in the rope (Figure 3), the horse is approached, and the end of the rope is taken over his neck and dropped through the loop in the slipknot in Figure 4.

Don't allow the end of the rope to come out of the loop as you pull hard on the other end. As you pull, the knot will twist and you'll produce the bowline as shown in Figure 5. With a little practice around the arm of a chair, a fence post, corral pole or hitchin' rail, you can have this knot down pat before ever trying it on a horse.

— *Chuck King*
Colorado Springs, Colorado

1.

2.

3.

4.

PULL HARD

5.

45

Clove Hitch and Bowline

WE'VE DONE a lot of camping at nearby state parks with our horses. Each camping spot has a hitch rail for campers to use. Since it's forbidden to tie to trees, we find ourselves leaving our horses tied to hitching rails for long periods of time.

CLOVE HITCH

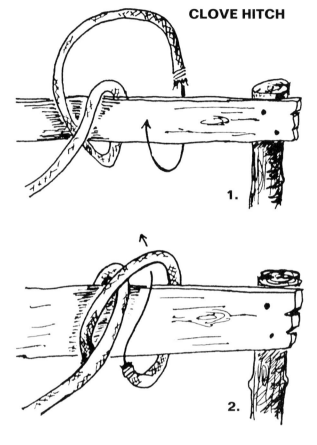

1.

2.

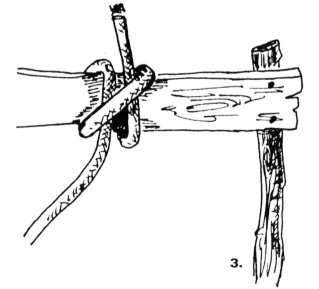

3.

It's not unusual on any given weekend to see other horses get loose, as well as tangled in their lead ropes. The biggest mistake people make is that they tie their horses with excess slack to enable them to eat off the ground. The horses sometimes get their feet over the ropes, or they're tied in such a manner that the rope slips down the post.

After trying all kinds of half hitches, slipknots and bowlines, I've settled on what I think is the best method for this situation. The first step is to tie a simple clove hitch in the middle of the hitch rail. This keeps the lead rope from sliding back and forth along the rail. I've found that just taking a couple of wraps works almost as well. The next step is to take the two ends that are left (one is hooked to the horse) and tie a bowline in it. This is a non-slip knot, and no matter how hard a horse pulls back, it's easy to untie.

— *Don Straight*
DeSoto, Iowa

BOWLINE

1.

2.

3.

4.

Sliding Knot

WHEN YOU have only a slick rope to use for a picket line, here's a way to tie the horse so he can't work his way up or down the line. But you can reposition the horse on the line without untying him.

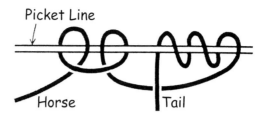

Tighten the wraps on the right hand by snugging them against the knot on the left. Roll the wraps around the line and pull the tail of the lead rope to tighten them. The horse can tug on his end of the lead, but won't be able to slide the knot up or down the picket line. Should you want to change the horse's position on the line, however, squeeze the entire knot together from both sides, and the knot easily slides to the desired spot.

— A.L. Devereux
Widener, Arkansas

Front Foot Tie-Up

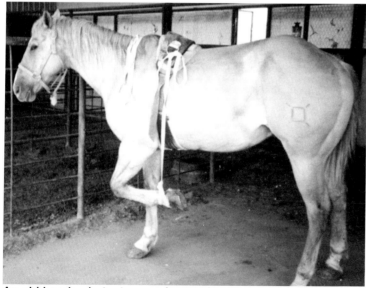

An old bareback rigging can be used to tie up a front foot of a horse that's difficult to shoe. This ranch horse is gentle ... except when he's being shod, so the rigging comes in handy.

SOME HORSES don't care to be shod. As a shoer, I had to find a way to tie up a front foot.

I've used a saddle, but that's too big to carry in the truck all of the time. I've tried figure-eight hobbles on the front legs too. I've also tried tying the horse's foot to his heart-girth area, but I still wasn't comfortable with the set-up, and I didn't have good access to the foot.

The solution: an old bareback rigging. I took the handle off and mounted a D-ring on each side. Using a cotton rope, I tied a front foot up to the rigging, and it worked great. First, I tied a bowline knot around the horse's pastern, then ran the rope through the ring in the rigging and tied it off with a quick-release knot.

I also have a honda in the other end of the rope for the horse who won't let you touch his foot, so you can rope it. The bareback rigging also works great for teaching a horse to lie down.

— Joe Wimberly
Millsap, Texas

Barn Safety Tie-Up

SAFELY TYING UP horses is a prime concern for all horse owners. Here's a neat set-up used by buckaroos in the horse barn at the Warm Springs Ranch near Eureka, Nev. This tie-up gives a horse some freedom of movement for eating, and you can move him over while saddling him, yet he can't become tangled in the lead rope. The danger of him pulling back is also reduced by the angle of the tie-up.

A rope is looped and tied with a square knot over a ceiling beam. A ring, such as an old cinch ring, is tied onto the other end using a bowline knot. The total length should be well above the point of a horse's shoulder. The halter lead rope can then be tied into the ring and daisy-chained to avoid a dangling end.

— *Mike Laughlin*
Eureka, Nevada

Snapless Lead Rope

ONE REASON rope halters are popular is because there is no hardware to break. So who wants to nullify this advantage by using a lead rope with a metal snap? However, a snap allows you to easily remove the lead rope when desired. As a compromise, here's a way to attach a lead rope without a snap, and it's still fairly easy to take the lead rope off when necessary.

1. Tie a loop in one end of your rope. A good knot to use when tying your loop is the double overhand knot. The construction of this knot is illustrated in "Build a Rope Halter" by Gayle Rieple, July 2002 *Western Horseman.*
2. Slip the loop in your lead rope over the double loops on your halter as shown in Figure 1.
3. Now pull the tail forward through the two halter loops.
4. Continue pulling until you have pulled the entire lead rope, including the loop knot, through the double halter loops.
5. Figure 2 shows the completed tie.
6. To remove, simply back the lead rope through the double halter loops.

Figure 1.   **Figure 2.**

— *Dale Fredricks*
Laredo, Texas

Mecate Knot

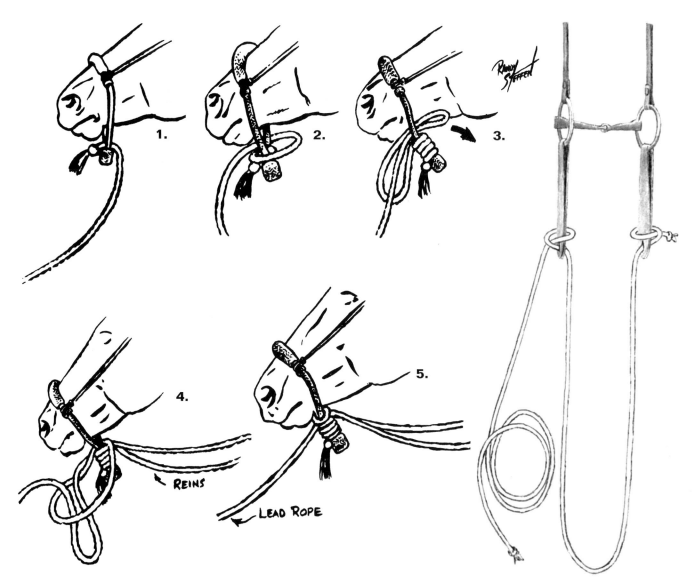

1.

2.

3.

4.

REINS

5.

LEAD ROPE

TO TIE THE MECATE, you need a hair rope (or other flexible rope about ⅝-inch in diameter) about 22 to 24 feet long. One end should have a Turk's-head knot and tassel. Follow these drawings step by step, adjusting your reins for proper length when you hit step 3, and you'll wind up with a workable set of reins and lead rope combined. Make as many wraps around the bosal as needed to make it fit correctly, but be careful not to make it too tight. The bosal should be loose enough to drop away from the jaws, giving relief from pressure, when the reins are slacked.

You can tuck the loose end of the lead rope under your belt so you can grab it if you have the misfortune of being bucked off. That way, your horse can't run off, leaving you afoot. Or, you can coil the lead rope and tie it on the near fork of your saddle until you need it.

Randy Steffen credited Ed Connell, author of *Hackamore Reinsman*, for showing him how to tie this knot. (Connell's book is still being sold by J.M. Capriola Co., 500 Commercial St., Elko, NV 89801; 702-738-5816.)

Many horsemen like to ride with a mecate and snaffle bit, using slobber straps to attach the mecate to the bit. Here's another illustration showing how to do that.

— *Randy Steffen*
Loomis, California

A Tie-Up Knot

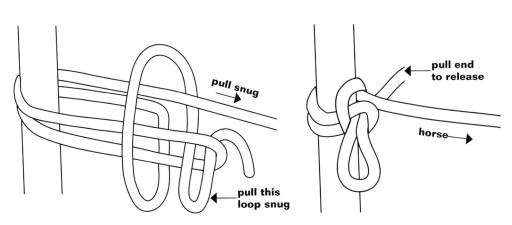

pull snug

pull this
loop snug

pull end
to release

horse

A FARRIER SHOWED ME this knot years ago, and I've used it exclusively ever since. Any pressure the animal applies isn't directly on the knot, so one quick yank and you're off like a bank robber.

— *Jed Greene*
Yreka, California

Jerk-Free Knot

JERK-
FREE
KNOT

NEAR AND
FRONT SIDE OF
DIAMOND

FROM
HALTER

1.

FREE
END OF
HALTER ROPE

2.

PULL
TO
TIGHTEN
KNOT

PULL
TO
TIGHTEN
KNOT

JERK
TO
RELEASE

3.

HERE'S A JERK-FREE, halter-rope knot that out-fitters use when working with large pack strings. They use it often, except on bad trails in timber where it might get snagged and jerked loose. But when driving a bunch of loose pack horses it's a handy and fast way to catch them. Sketches 1, 2 and 3 show how the free end of the halter rope is tucked under the diamond hitch to form the jerk-free knot.

— *Chuck King*
Colorado Springs, Colorado

Highline Prussic Knot

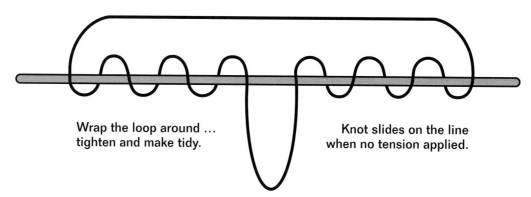

Wrap the loop around ...
tighten and make tidy.

Knot slides on the line
when no tension applied.

WE'RE ALWAYS on the lookout for innovative ideas that can make our backcountry trips more efficient. We've found that using a "prussic knot" (see photo) to attach metal swivels to our highline works well for us. The prussic knot can slide along the highline when there isn't tension on the knot, but it stays firmly in place on the line when tension is applied by hitching a horse to the swivel.

In order to minimize the length of time that our horses need to be tied to trees when we first arrive at our campsite, we try to set up our highline as soon as possible. With our swivels preattached to our highline (a 50-foot, lightweight, 1-inch nylon tube strapping) by the use of a prussic knot, we can quickly connect each end of the highline to a tree saver, tighten the line and adjust the spacing to suit the situation. The ideal feature of the prussic-knot method is the fact that a person can adjust the swivel positions without loosening the highline.

As shown here, a strong metal swivel is attached to the highline with a ⅜-inch, three-strand, nylon rope, back-spliced to form a loop of approximately 9 inches. Having a swivel attached to the highline eliminates the need to use a lead rope with a heavy swivel snap. It's necessary to have a swivel somewhere in the connection to prevent the lead rope from being unwound by a horse who moves around in circles while tied to the highline.

— Edd Blackler
Bigfork, Montana

Hackamore Tie

YOU CAN TRANSFORM a hackamore into a halter in a few easy steps. Bring the doubled rein to one side of the horse's neck, then take it over the neck, near the throatlatch. Catch the tail, bringing it under and then wrapping it over the doubled rein, with the loop positioned near the knot of the bosal. Bring the end of the mecate through the loop. You can take up more slack by taking more wraps.

— Jack Swanson
Carmel Village, California

JNS

Lead-Rope Cavalry Knot

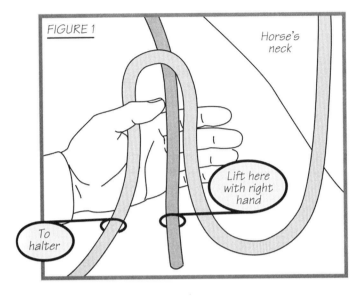

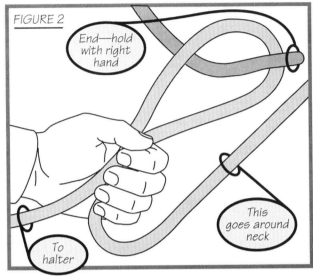

OUT ON THE TRAIL you sometimes want to get off your horse and tie up. You can ride with your halter under your bridle, but securing the lead rope to the saddle can be a problem.

Here's an easy way to solve the problem. It's similar to what cavalrymen did. Just observe the easy steps that follow.

Look at Figure 1. For now, leave the lead attached to the halter. Standing on the left (near) side of your horse, grasp the rope with your left hand. Slide your hand from the halter connection to an area near the base of the neck. With your right hand pass the free end of the rope over the horse's neck. Bring it under the neck from the other side, and under the portion of the rope held in the left hand. Using the free end, which is in your right hand, raise both pieces of rope at the point where they cross. This causes a loop to form in the left hand.

Close the left hand around that loop. Tilt the left fist forward, causing a second loop to be formed around the knuckles, as in Figure 2. Now grasp all three pieces of the rope, which form the two loops, in the left hand. You now have a bundle of three strands, with a loop on each end, as illustrated in Figure 3.

The end of the lead rope is already through the top loop. Begin wrapping the end under, then back over the top of the bundle of ropes. This is also shown in Figure 3. Continue until most of the lead rope is wrapped snugly

Here's what the completed halter-and-lead-rope arrangement looks like. You can put the bridle over the halter as you ride, or you can stuff the halter in a saddlebag and clip the lead rope to a D-ring on the saddle,

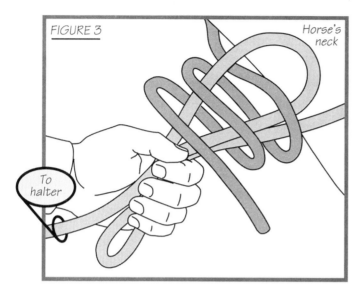

FIGURE 3

Horse's neck

To halter

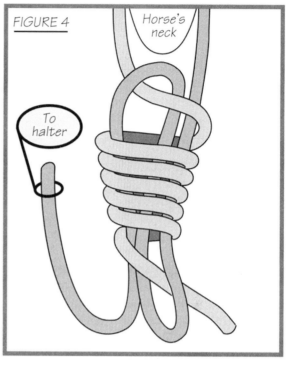

FIGURE 4

Horse's neck

To halter

around the bundle. After the last wrap, tuck the rope through the bottom loop. Pull everything snug. Now the knot should look like Figure 4.

Hold the knot with one hand. Now tug on the rope leading to the halter. Next tug on the rope going over the horse's neck, on the near side. This will tighten the knot and cause it to look like Figure 5 when completed.

Do not overtighten. That will make it hard to untie. It needs to be only snug enough to keep it together. The end should be left a little longer than indicated in Figure 5. The weight of a longer end will keep it in the loop better.

The knot in Figure 5 is snugged and ready to go. If all the adjustments are correct, it will hang correctly, as shown in the photograph.

To untie the knot, grasp the bottom loop in one hand and the knot in the other. Work the loop out enough to pull the free end back through it, then simply unwrap the coils. The knot will fall apart.

Although some riders leave the lead rope snapped to the halter, others prefer to snap it to a D-ring on the saddle as a safety measure. This eliminates the loop from the halter ring to the knot around the horse's neck. This loop can snag on brush, or a horse can stick a front foot through it when he bends down to drink at a stream or munch some grass.

— *Gary D. Kirchmeier*
Cave Creek, Arizona

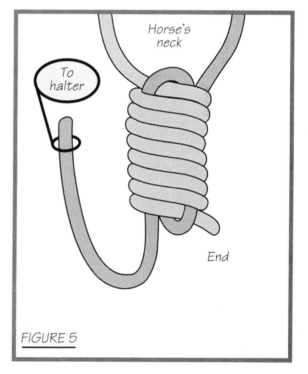

Horse's neck

To halter

End

FIGURE 5

6 TRAILERS AND HAULING HORSES

Overhead Trailer Picket Line

AT HORSE SHOWS, trail rides or just about any other kind of activity, you'll notice quite a few ways of taking care of horses. Of course, you might luck out once in a while and find stalls or small corrals for rent, but usually the trailer becomes home for your horses, and they sure will head right for it when the ride or competition is over.

Although the most common method is tying horses directly to the trailer, it has some faults, including the horse getting a foot tangled in the tires, lights, braces, etc. Portable corrals are becoming more common, and there are several other good ways to confine your horse and still keep him fairly comfortable and safe.

But one of the best tricks is the overhead picket line, stretched between two trailers. Depending on how far apart the trailers are positioned, quite a few horses can be secured in this way, and they have some freedom of movement — more than if they were tied to the trailer. Also, there's less chance of them getting tangled up in the lead rope, or somewhere in the trailer.

Hanging a hay net in front of the horses helps keep them occupied, and if they're inclined to fight with the horses next to them, a couple of squabbles will teach them to stay out of kicking range. Or a kicker can be tied on the far side of the trailer.

Grain can be fed in nosebags, or by dumping the water bucket long enough for the horse to clean up his oats.

— *Gary Vorhes*
Peyton, Colorado

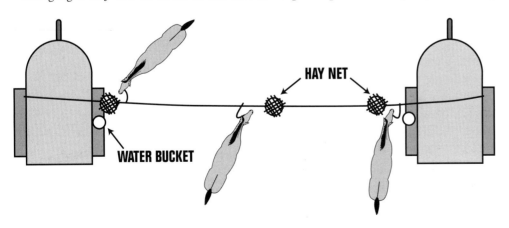

HAY NET

WATER BUCKET

Tiedown Tip

I SOMETIMES have to load and haul horses by myself. Occasionally I need an extra hand to hold open the trailer door while loading. If I have to park on an uphill grade, it's difficult to keep the door fully open and out of the way. And, more times than I care to remember, a blast of wind has blown the trailer door partially closed while my horse was stepping in or out.

I use a bungee cord as my extra hand. I attach one end of the cord to the door and the other to the side of the trailer. After I load the horse, I can quickly unhook the cord and close the door.

Depending on the distance, you might have to use two cords hooked securely together, in order to stretch far enough. You can purchase bungee cords of varying lengths at hardware stores.

— Martha Branon Holden
Yadkinville, North Carolina

VINTAGE — Horseman's Scrapbook

Flat-Tire Ramp

Here's an easy way to change a flat tire on a trailer. Bevel a section of 6-inch beam, as shown, to provide a ramp to raise the wheel off the ground for removal. This method is easier than using a jack, and it'll work on either the front or the rear axle.

— Randy Steffen

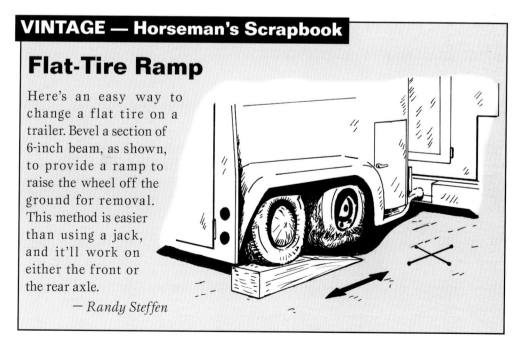

Star-Wrench Storage

IF YOU PULL a horse trailer, chances are your trailer and truck tires have different size lug nuts. In case of an emergency, you need a wrench for each size of lug nut.

The solution many haulers choose is a star wrench. It has four sockets, and you should be able to find one to fit each vehicle's lugs. In the case of 1-ton trucks and RVs, you might even need to buy a larger size wrench. These wrenches are easier to use than the ones that come with your vehicle, and they provide more leverage on tight nuts.

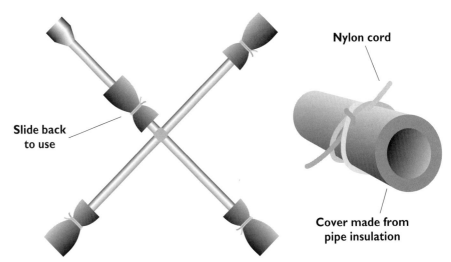

Nylon cord

Slide back to use

Cover made from pipe insulation

Everything has its drawbacks, and star wrenches are no exception. They're clumsy to carry. The most efficient way to transport them is in the vertical position. Whether you carry them in your tack compartment or behind your truck's seat, vertical is best. In the vertical position though, they flop back and forth and make a lot of noise.

To alleviate that problem, buy some foam pipe insulation. You can find it in most hardware stores, in short lengths of 3 to 4 feet. Cut off four 5-inch pieces. Slide one over each star wrench socket. Tie a 30-inch piece of parachute cord around the insulation.

The illustration shows the cord tied around the insulation in a clove hitch. If you don't know how to tie a clove hitch, just wrap the cord around twice and tie a square knot. Tie the cord toward the inside, between the socket and the middle of the wrench. Pull it as tight as possible. Cut off the excess cord. You can use plastic tie wraps instead of the cord.

Slide the foam back away from the socket to use it, then slide it back over the wrench end to cushion it for storage. You'll have a much quieter trip with this arrangement.

— Gary D. Kirchmeier
Cave Creek, Arizona

The Bumper Bumper

IF YOUR TOW vehicle has a fancy chrome bumper or delicate fiberglass roll pan, you know how careful you need to be when hooking up your horse trailer — especially if you don't have a friend to yell "Stop!" as you back up. It's easy to mar a perfectly good day and bumper by connecting truck and trailer at the wrong height.

Here's a cheap and easy way to avoid hitching anxiety. Buy a foam can cover (sold to keep soda and beer cans cool) and slip it over your hitch before backing. The soft foam will cushion your hitch to keep it from scratching or denting the bumper as you position the trailer ball under the coupling. For about a dollar, you've saved your temper and your bumper.

— Suzanne Drnec
Chino, California

Portable Tack Room

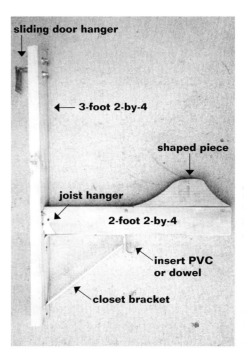

TO KEEP saddles off the ground or out of the back of my pickup while at horse shows, I developed this portable tack-room arrangement for the side of a horse trailer. And it works well when you have a tack stall at shows. The long rod can be used to hang clothes, too, just like a closet.

You'll need:
1   2-by-4, 3 feet long
1   2-by-4, 2 feet long
1   closet bracket
1   joist hanger for 2-by-4
1   sliding-door hanger
1   shaped wooden piece to hold saddle
1   1-inch diameter PVC pipe or wooden dowel, length to suit
bolts and nails for above hardware

— *Frank Dryden*
Monument, Colorado

Weanlings in a Two-Horse Trailer

PEOPLE OFTEN buy weanling horses that've been halter-broke, but have never been in trailer. Then, they must haul the young horses home at the time of purchase, without having the opportunity to train them to the trailer.

Probably, the best way to haul a colt or filly is by turning it loose in a stock trailer. But many people only have a two-horse trailer, and they find that young horses tend to try to climb into the manger.

To minimize this problem, tie a partial bale of straw or hay in the manger, being careful to pack it in tightly and remove all loose wires that might cause injury. The bale blocks the windows and fills the manager, discouraging the young horse from trying to jump into it.

Next, tie a lead rope to the halter and to the tie ring at the front of the trailer, being careful to leave enough rope for the horse to feel the butt chain or butt bar before he feels the pull of the rope, thus stopping any fighting. The rope prevents the horse from getting turned around.

— *Lynda Layne*
Winchester Bay, Oregon

Self-Taught Trailer Loading

MANY HORSEMEN believe in training a foal early. Here's a hint that should be useful to the backyard horse owner — a simple, temporary creep-feeder used in combination with a method for teaching the foal to load into a trailer.

The diagram shows two 12-by-12-feet stalls. The wall between these stalls consists of 11 2-by-8-inch boards that drop into slots formed by 2-by-2-inch strips nailed approximately 2 inches apart. When the mare is ready to foal, the 2-by-8s can be easily removed, making a 12-by-24-foot foaling stall. Spread a thick layer of straw bedding on the floor.

When the foal is big enough to eat hay and grain, place a single 2-by-8 between the stalls at a height that allows the foal to enter the creep-feed stall, but low enough to keep out the mare. The diagram shows this arrangement; two small blocks of wood nailed between the 2-by-2-inch strips keep the dividing board in place. This is necessary because the greedy mare might learn to duck under the rail and lift it. The height of this rail can be adjusted as the foal grows.

The diagram shows a horse trailer backed up to the foal's corral. Provide a ramp with bedding straw to help the foal take that first step into the trailer. Put a pan of oats on the trailer floor and keep moving it back until the foal loads into the trailer to eat his oats. Eventually, he'll eat out of the manger in the trailer. During this process, gradually remove the straw from the ramp until the colt takes the big step into the trailer. I've trained a couple of colts this way, and it beats loading lessons. With this method, the colt teaches himself to load. If you can spare a trailer for this, it sure works.

The diagram also shows a gate in the mare's corral; keep it open, and the mare and foal have the run of the pasture. We weaned our colt last November, and he's stabled in what used to be his creep-feed stall. We've replaced the 2-by-8s, and he now has his own stall. I'd hesitate to call any procedure with horses foolproof — there are too many variables; but if there's a drawback to this training method, I have yet to find it.

— *Chan Bergen*
Colorado Springs, Colorado

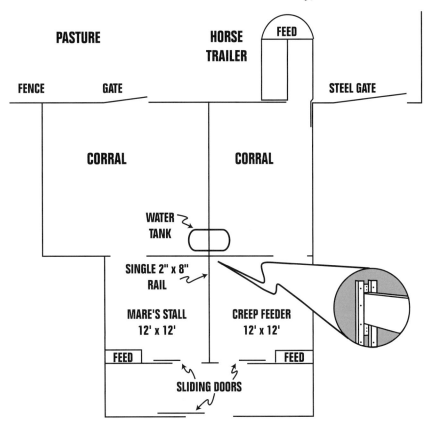

Bungee Cord Hitch-Finder

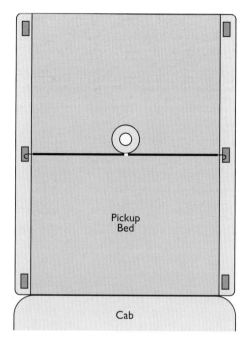

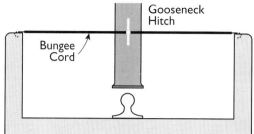

TO ALIGN THE gooseneck hitch with the ball on the trailer, I use a system that's cheap, easy and requires very little storage space. I drive a truck with a long wheelbase. I stretch a bungee cord from the center side rail pocket to the same pocket on the other side, and the bungee cord crosses the hitch ball. I then connect the trailer, paint a white mark on the bungee cord and a white mark on the gooseneck. The next time I hook up the trailer, I simply back up and align the marks. When the bungee cord moves, the ball and the hitch are perfectly aligned. You can remove the bungee cord and store it in very little space.

— Jim Rothfeldt
High Springs, Florida

Horse-Trailer Sling

THE "EASY HAULER" — the horse that's trained to load, unload and haul without any problems — is always a pleasure to transport. But occasionally, I've had a real scrambler on my hands. A scrambler might load and unload fine, but as soon as the trailer moves, he leans into the center divider and tries to climb the walls. While scrambling, the horse might lose his balance and go down, with the possibility of injury.

To solve this problem, I build a temporary sling inside the trailer, with two wide cinches and a hefty length of rope. If you have a stock trailer, you can probably use the rope to attach each cinch to the vertical bars in the trailer wall and center divider. If you have a standard solid-wall trailer, you need to weld two rings to the trailer wall and two rings to the divider. You can then tie the cinches to these rings. (**Editor's note:** *Make sure the center divider in your particular trailer is strong enough to support the weight of a horse.*)

The cinches fit up under the horse's body, in about the same locations as the front and rear cinches of a saddle. They should be snug up against the horse's belly so that he can feel the support. If the horse gets nervous, spooks, or loses his balance while the trailer is moving, the sling will catch him and prevent him from climbing the walls or going down.

— Kenneth Whitlow
Yamhill, Oregon

Tire-Changing Aid

YOU'RE DRIVING along hauling horses in your twin-axle trailer. Suddenly a trailer tire goes flat. Everyone who hauls horses someday faces this situation.

There's an easy way to solve this problem without unloading your horses along the highway, which is often dangerous. Another plus is that you don't have to wrestle with a heavy jack or crawl around under the trailer getting the jack in position.

Find some scrap lumber. You need three 2-by-6-inch pieces 25 inches long, four 2-by-4-inch pieces 17 inches long to lay crosswise over the first layer, and on top of that you need four 2-by-4-inch pieces 16 inches long to put crossways on the second layer.

Look at the photos to get the idea. You can vary the sizes or lengths according to what's on hand, but you need three layers stair-stepping. Nail or screw the whole works together.

To use your new aid, position it ahead or behind the tire that's not flat. Loosen the lug bolts on the flat tire, then drive or back the trailer to position the good tire on top of the aid.

Block the wheels on the opposite side of the trailer. Remove the flat tire, put the spare on the wheel, snug the lug bolts up, unblock the far-side wheels, move the trailer off the aid and finish tightening the lug bolts.

You can also use the pad under the trailer jack when you unhook the trailer. When the ground is soft or snowy, the block will keep the jack from sinking or freezing down. You can also use the block to change tires on dual-rear-wheel pickups or RVs.

— *Mike Laughlin*
Eureka, Nevada

Door Grill for Trailers

IF YOU LIVE in a hot climate, you want plenty of ventilation in your horse trailer. Here's how to alter a two-horse trailer with solid top doors. Have a welding shop make grill-type doors out of square tubing. Make the corners on the doors with 1-inch tubing, and the vertical pieces out of ½-inch sections. In the configuration shown, the grilled doors are welded to the middle doors above the ramp. That way they close at the same time, speeding up the process.

The grill allows much more air to circulate through the trailer and is very attractive. This grill would also be an excellent addition to step-up trailers that are made with one-piece doors and no top doors.

— *Lynda Layne*
Winchester Bay, Oregon

Hitch Hook

A SIMPLE, INEXPENSIVE tool can make fastening a goose-neck trailer hitch with a D-shaped handle an easy chore.

Use at least a 4-foot section of ¾-inch electric wall conduit. Put about 4 inches of the conduit into a vise, and squeeze the conduit as flat as possible. Then, with about 2 inches of the flattened conduit in the vise, bend the rest of it at a 90-degree angle to form a hook on one end.

Use the conduit hook to latch or unlatch the trailer hitch. This also is a great tool to carry in your truck so you can reach a cooler or toolbox without climbing into the truck bed.

One 10-foot piece of pipe costs about $3 and makes two hooker sticks.

— William Blackman
Fayetteville, North Carolina

Trailering Warning

IN WARM WEATHER, it's not unusual to see slant-load trailers with drop windows going down the highway with the horses hanging out their heads. True, it's cooler for the horses, but it's very dangerous! A horse can lose an eye to a rock kicked up by a passing vehicle (just as windshields get cracked by flying rocks); an insect can fly into an eye; the wind can cause eye problems; or, worst of all, the horse can suffer severe and possibly fatal head injuries if he's struck by a passing vehicle, such as a big semi, or even by the rear-view mirror on a large truck.

If you must leave the windows down in hot weather, install some type of screen or guard so the horses must keep their heads inside. Some trailer dealers can have the coverings made for you. Also, many trailer manufacturers install grille guards.

— Pat Close
Elizabeth, Colorado

7 TRAIL RIDING AND BACKCOUNTRY CAMPING

Stock-Handling Tips

USE AS FEW head of stock on a pack trip as possible. A pack animal can carry about 20 percent of his body weight. So minimize the load by repackaging food items, etc., in lightweight containers, and make the most of each animal's carrying capacity.

For some parts of the forest already showing signs of heavy use keep the impact from stock in the same spot, rather than moving them around every day. However, the one-place, one-impact school of thought doesn't apply to all areas. Check with the Forest Service in a given location to find out if livestock should be spread around or more confined.

Allow your pack animals to graze a large area first and get their fill before confining them behind an electric fence. A portable electric fence is easy to use and light to pack. The batteries of some varieties last as long as 3 weeks. The important thing is to accustom your livestock to an electric fence at home, before you hit the trail.

If you stake-out livestock, move the picket pin frequently to prevent heavy environmental wear. If you can see a circle around the picket pin, you're too late in moving your stock.

For information on leave-no-trace, low-impact camping, call 800-332-4100. The Forest Service provides information about traveling in the wilderness with stock. Check telephone listings under U.S. Government, Department of Agriculture, for the U.S. Forest Service, or look under the listing Federal Agencies. Forest Service offices have contact information for other forest areas.

— *Fran Devereux Smith*
Peyton, Colorado

Bag Tree-Saver

WHEN YOU'RE CLEANING the tack room, don't throw away those old burlap bags. And if you see any at a garage sale or an auction, buy them.

As federal, state and local managers put more and more restrictions on high-lining picket lines or just tying single horses to trees, a few of these bags in your trailer can be mighty handy.

The heavy burlap makes an excellent substitute for other kinds of tree-savers. Simply fold a couple of sacks in fourths, place them against the tree and then tie the rope over the bags. They protect the bark from scarring, and keep any official who wanders by happy that you're complying with the rules.

— *Bonnie Davis*
Fremont, California

VINTAGE — Horseman's Scrapbook

Tail Lights

This hint might cause a snicker or two at first glance, but if you live in a heavily populated area where traffic is fast and furious, and if you have occasion to ride along busy streets after dark, don't take this lightly. It could prevent an accident to you and your horse. A reader who lives in California participates in quite a few parades and other horse activities after dark. Her "tail light" rig is practical and easy to use. Made from a piece of white cloth or canvas, with rings to attach to the saddle strings, it features a row of small red reflectors around the cloth that pick up and reflect the head-lights of traffic from the rear and both sides.

— *Randy Steffen*

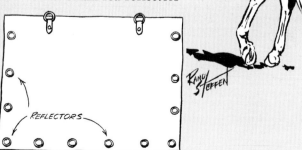

REFLECTORS

No Surprises

WHEN YOU'RE BEDDING DOWN on the ground at night, out on the range, here's a good old-fashioned hint on how to keep from finding "surprises" in your boots the next morning. Ever since trail-driving days, cowboys have

SCOTT MILLER

enlivened the campfire conversations with tales of the various varmints that've crawled into their boots at night seeking warmth. The usual tales range from scorpions, tarantulas, red snakes — and it's a real greenhorn who pulls on his boots in the morning without turning them upside down and thumping the soles a time or two.

This old method cuts down on your chances of having company in your boots when you pull them on. When you take them off at night, simply stuff the top of one boot inside the other. Even with this precaution, most old-timers will still turn 'em over and thump 'em before slipping their feet down inside.

— *Dick Spencer*
Colorado Springs, Colorado

True South

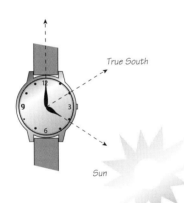

True South

Sun

IF YOU don't have a compass handy, you can use a wristwatch to establish your direction. Digital watches won't work; use a watch with an hour hand and one set for the correct time.

It's easier to get your bearings if you take off the watch and hold it in your hand. Point the hour hand toward the sun, wherever that may be. The point halfway between the hour hand and the 12 on the watch is true south.

— *Bob Lantis*
Rapid City, South Dakota

Nose Bags

THESE MESH NOSEBAGS are very durable. The mesh is fine enough to retain the feed, but large enough that, if a horse tries to drink while wearing the bag, the water flows out instantly, making it impossible for the horse to drown.

The material, available from tent and awning companies, is synthetic fiber mesh and is most commonly used as a trucker's tarp. Grommets and a strong carpet thread are all that is required to make the bag.

Aside from their strength and safety, these bags fold flat and take up very little room — an asset to a packer.

— *Debby Miller*
Thousand Oaks, California

Salt-Block Packs

A RANCHER friend of mine complained to me that he has problems getting salt and mineral blocks out of panniers. Most panniers are cone-shaped. With some design modification, I came up with an easy-to-load-and-unload device that's easy to hook onto a packsaddle. This contraption works very well and is made of recycled material.

— *Hellmut Patzelt*
Dawson Creek, British Columbia

Tent-Stove Safety

HERE'S A SAFETY HINT for anyone packing into the high country in cold weather and who uses a wood stove in a wall tent. If you run the stovepipe straight up through the roof, sparks fall on the canvas and cause a fire danger, not to mention holes that leak rain.

It's much safer to use pipe with an adjustable-angle section and run it out through the front "door" at a 45-degree angle. With the front of the tent facing with the wind, sparks are carried away from the tent. I think you could also use this same setup with range tepee tents.

It's nice to return to a warm, dry tent after a day of hunting or fishing, not to mention the joy you'll feel on a raw, cold morning when you can reach out with one hand, stuff some fire-starter and kindling in the stove, scratch a match and snuggle back in your bedroll while the tent warms up. And if you were smart the evening before, the coffee pot starts to boil. Coffee in bed? You bet! I also sew a light clothesline into the peak of the tent to hang socks, etc. to dry.

But you have to be careful with fire in a tent. I've had big holes appear in two of my tents, one from sparks, and one caused by a mosquito coil, the kind you burn that kills the little beasts. It was by the canvas door, the wind blew the door into the coil, and although the door never burst into flame, it didn't take long for a hole to glow into an opening 3 feet by 3 feet. The bugs had a feast that trip, and Alaska's mosquitoes are more feared than her bears.

— *Richard M. Barnes*
Fairbanks, Alaska

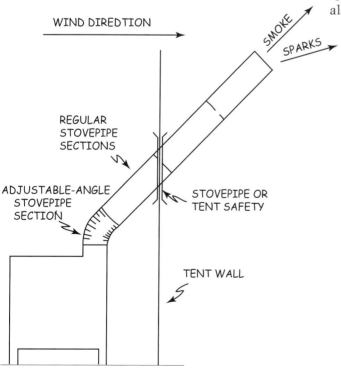

WIND DIREDTION

SMOKE

SPARKS

REGULAR
STOVEPIPE
SECTIONS

ADJUSTABLE-ANGLE
STOVEPIPE
SECTION

STOVEPIPE OR
TENT SAFETY

TENT WALL

No-Board Decker Packsaddle

OVER THE YEARS I've relied on horses and mules to assist me in my livelihood of packing, looking after cattle and hillside farming in some of the steepest, most rugged and remote country of the Northwest — Hells Canyon of the Snake River in the northeast corner of Oregon. So I feel an obligation to help out the pack animals a little bit. In the back-country a person is so dependent on his horses and mules that he becomes quite sensitive to their welfare.

Good, well-fitted and padded saddles and harnesses are necessities to prevent sores and galls. That's why I discourage the use of boards in the half-breed saddle covers on Decker packsaddles.

Originally the idea began with the old Arapaho saddle that had no tree and was a large, stuffed pad molded to fit the individual animal. Loads were slung on and secured by going around the bottom of the half-breeds, where a stick was placed in the bottom to provide some stability.

Some of the first Decker half-breeds had much wider boards to distribute the bearing weight of loads that included small mining equipment or farm machinery. Another purpose of the boards was to minimize wear on the canvas cover. But as time progressed, such loads were no longer packed, and the boards became narrower, which made the saddle lighter and easier to use.

Today loads are most frequently packed in panniers or mantied with a bearing space of approximately 2 square feet. With the boards in the half-breed under-neath these types of loads, there's a weight-bearing area of 96 square inches as compared to about 400 square inches without the boards.

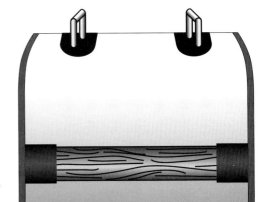

A half-breed cover with board.

A half-breed cover with wear-leather and padded with tail hair.

Loaded or empty, using boards under a tight rigging still causes sores on a pack animal's sides. But the old-style, slab-sided mules of yesteryear tolerated the use of boards better than the rib-sprung animals of today. Modern packsaddle trees have been modified to fit the modern animal's back. So why not modify things to help out the poor old rib cage?

I put a large wear-leather in place of the boards to mini-mize wear on the half-breed, and I also stuff the half-breed with tail hair, bear grass or felt pads 2 to 3 inches thick. With this method I've never had side sores or gall marks on my pack animals, and this method also holds the load out and away from the hipbones and shoulders.

I don't recommend foam rubber for stuffing as it deteri-orates with hard use, holds moisture and, due to its buoyancy, makes it hard to keep the cinch tight. Tail hair is best since it's light, holds its loftiness and doesn't retain moisture or wear out. Tail hair and bear grass conform to an animal's back over time and give much support to the load the ani-mal carries.

Just look at the white marks on your animals, and when they're loaded, notice where the bearing point of the load falls. I hope the weight isn't bearing on little 1-by-4-inch boards or an old ax handle, as I've seen used many times.

— *Fred Talbott*
Union, Oregon

The marks on the mule show the results of using boards in the half-breed cover on a Decker packsaddle.

Power Saw Carrier

THIS WOODEN CRADLE fits onto a Decker packsaddle. It accommodates the power saw, a gas container, oil and hand tools. The cradle, axe, saw and container are held securely by two seatbelts that have about 3 inches of heavy-duty elastic sewn into them on the offside.

— *Hellmut Patzelt*
Dawson Creek, British Columbia

Low-Tech Nosebag

FEEDING IN A NOSEBAG is extremely handy. There's no waste and you're sure that the most timid horse gets his share. Here's about the most economical type of bag I've seen. If you have an old gunny sack and can cut a strip of rubber from an inner tube, and tie a couple of square or double-overhand knots, you can make your own.

— *Gary Vorhes*
Peyton, Colorado

Seat-Belt Tree-Savers

FOLKS WHO RIDE IN national and state forests and parks are familiar with tree-saver straps. To prevent damage, these broad bands are fastened around a tree, with a horse tied to a loop or ring on the band, rather than being tied directly to the tree.

Here's a tip that supports both low-impact packing and recycling as well: Make your own tree-saver straps from used seat-belts. You can find them at a junk yard. Just strip them from vehicles and sew the buckle end and the receiver end together. A shoe shop can sew them, if you can't.

But before you sew them together, run the seat-belt through a ring for the lead rope or picket rope. Or, just braid a loop in some rope and run the seat belt through it.

Either way, the used seat-belts are adjustable and easy to fasten around a tree. They're good, solid nylon with buckles and are the right width to distribute the pressure.

— *Fran Devereux Smith*
Peyton, Colorado

Backcountry Hitching Post

THIS TIP comes courtesy of Bob Landis of Gunsel Horse Adventures near Rapid City, S.D. When there's no hitching post available in the backcountry, here's how to tie pack and riding stock. Saddle two horses, then tie them head-to-tail. The pair can move around in a limited circle, but find it difficult to leave the campsite. Tie the riding horse's lead rope to the back of the sawbuck packsaddle. Then tie the pack horse's lead to the saddle horn or a back dee on the saddle.

— *Fran Devereux Smith*
Peyton, Colorado

Snap Links

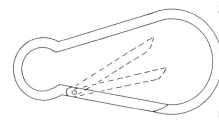

SNAP LINKS ARE handy for a variety of applications where strength isn't a factor. A pair of these can convert two stakeout cuffs into hobbles.

You can use an old saddle cinch, with a link snapped into one end, as a lash cinch. You can also snap a pair into the cinch rings of a packsaddle to make handy sling rings for manteed loads.

— *Al Huseby*
Eyota, Minnesota

Pack-Horse Hobbles

HOBBLES ARE HANDY anytime, but especially for pack animals. To adjust a pack, keep stock from wandering off or if you're packing up at a spot where there isn't anything to tie to, the answer is to hobble the animal.

Here's a way to have hobbles always handy and to use them as a tie-down in the meantime. One end loops around the breast collar and the other around the throatlatch of the halter.

— *Mike Laughlin*
Eureka, Nevada

Camping Duffel Bag

TO CREATE THIS easy-to-make duffel bag, simply obtain an old denim skirt. Cut a circle out of old denim to fit in the top of the waist band and top stitch it in. A drawstring isn't necessary when it's used for blankets or pillows. A drawstring may be put into the hem of the skirt when the duffel bag is used for smaller gear.

— Jo Schaaf
Atkinson, Nebraska

OPTIONAL DRAWSTRING

PIECE OF OLD DENIM

Packing Tips

HERE ARE SOME TIPS from forest rangers that can help recreational packers match their expectations with the experience they want to have.

Foremost is planning where to pack, how best to package the load and when to make the trip.

Areas described as "wilderness" draw many hikers, campers and packers. Other Forest Service areas open for recreation, but not specifically designated as wilderness areas, often are underutilized and have much to offer. It's a good idea, though, to call the Forest Service office in advance. To spread the impact of recreational users in his area, a ranger might suggest a trail less traveled, but equally entertaining to ride.

The less you bring into an area, the less impact, and this requires good planning. Foodstuffs, especially those packaged in liquid in jars, tend to test a packer's weight and space limitations. By repackaging such foods in lighter-weight containers, you lighten the load. This, in turn, can mean fewer head of stock to pack or that you use the on-hand stock more efficiently. On a trip for several people and lasting several days, repackaging groceries can make many pounds of difference in the load.

Last-minute considerations in making a successful pack trip include weather, fire and trail conditions or closings. Unfortunately, unpredictable conditions can ruin the best plans. However, you can usually get up-to-date information by making a phone call or two. Again, an area ranger might suggest an alternate camp or trail, so you don't lose out on your trip altogether.

— Fran Devereux Smith
Peyton, Colorado

Safety Considerations

HERE ARE SOME SAFETY tips for novice packers.

1. Don't duck under your livestock's neck when you're packing a load. You'll only get run over should your pack animal spook and jump forward. Instead, move from side to side by walking around the animal.
2. When it's necessary to work around a pack animal's rear end, move in close to his body. He may try to kick you, but because you're standing close, you won't get the full brunt of the blow.
3. Watch your feet to keep from getting stepped on.
4. Don't drop the lash rope on the ground. It's easy to tangle a foot in it, and that can cause major problems should something spook your pack animal.

5. The safest way to work around your pack animal when reaching under his belly for a cinch is to face forward. A pack animal may try to kick you, but will be less likely to hit you in the head when you're facing forward.

— *Fran Devereux Smith*
Peyton, Colorado

Packsaddle Tips

THIS TIP comes courtesy of Bob Landis of Gunsel Horse Adventures near Rapid City, S.D. When putting a packsaddle on your horse or mule, be sure to pull the blankets or pads well up into the gullet of the sawbuck, where it rests over the withers. Then, when you cinch up, the blankets won't pull tightly against the skin at the withers, which can be uncomfortable to the animal.

Once you load the sawbuck, it's important to put the lash cinch between the connecting strap (joining the packsaddle cinches) and the horse or mule's belly. Otherwise, when you tie down the load, the lash cinch mashes the connector into the animal's soft underbelly.

— *Fran Devereux Smith*
Peyton, Colorado

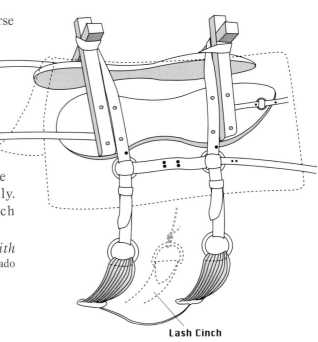

Lash Cinch

Single Hobble Construction

A HOBBLE FOR one leg is a useful tool to have in your tack room or horse trailer. Many horsemen think it's best to picket a horse by a front leg, using a swivel stake and a single hobble. Some riders like to use full hobbles on both front legs, and a sideline to a back leg. This requires a single hobble for the back leg. You can also combine two single hobbles and a short chain to make a full set of hobbles.

But, a single hobble is usually hard to find. Here's an easy way to make one.

The illustration depicts a finished hobble. The materials required are as follows:

Mark through outside

1 length of harness leather 32 inches long by 1½ inches wide
1 2-inch roller buckle
1 2-inch D-ring
1 rivet

The leather should be about ¼-inch thick, and should be well-oiled. A saddlemaker will probably have harness leather available. Substitutes can be found in most tack rooms, such as an old billet from a western saddle. Other substitutes might include a cinch latigo or a discarded flank cinch. If a substitute is used, it should be in good condition, strong and well-oiled for comfort.

The buckle and D-ring should be malleable iron. Avoid pot-metal hardware. Poor quality metal is hard to detect, so acquire hardware from a reliable source. The rivet can be a copper rivet or a Chicago screw. A leather thong may be substituted for the rivet. Its sole purpose is to keep things together when the hobble is unbuckled.

Double the leather, and cut a slot for the tongue of the buckle in the middle. The slot should be centered on the leather and have a rough dimension of ¾-inch-long by ¼-inch-wide. Install the buckle and D-ring as shown in the illustration. Punch a hole and install the rivet about 2 inches back from the tongue of the buckle. Measure 9 inches from the tongue, and punch a hole at 10 inches, and one at 11 inches. At this point there should be three holes in the outside 1-inch apart. More may be added if needed.

The holes in both layers of leather won't line up, in use, if they're punched at the same time. It's necessary to wrap the hobble around something the size of your horse's leg, and mark the second layer of leather through the holes in the outside layer. Try wrapping it around a human wrist to mark it.

The dimensions given here are only guidelines. Horses vary in size, and availability of material might vary greatly. Use common sense with substitute materials, and if you're unfamiliar with hobbles, consult a trainer before using them.

— *Gary D. Kirchmeier*
Cave Creek, Arizona

BARN EQUIPMENT

Drop-Down Saddle Rack

JULIE GOODNIGHT of the Certified Horsemanship Association provided this tip. Here's a handy idea that helps keep your saddle out of the dirt when your hitching post isn't close to the tack-room door.

Fasten simple drop-down saddle racks at each end of your hitch rails and on posts around the barn.

Make each rack of 4-by-4-inch lumber cut long enough to accommodate a saddle. The hook-and-eye bolt you use for each rack are inexpensive and easy to find at local hardware or discount stores.

To use the rack, insert the hook through the eye bolt from underneath so the end of the rack is braced against the post.

To drop the rack down and flush against the post, bring the hook through the eye bolt from the top.

Drill a hole at a convenient height in the post where you want a rack, and fasten the eye bolt there. Then use screws to attach the hook to one edge of the 4-by-4 rack as shown in the photographs.

To hang a saddle, insert hook from underneath the eye bolt. The end of the rack braces against the post so the rack remains stable when you place a saddle on it. Once you've saddled up, unhook the rack and rehang it, bringing the hook down through the eye. Now the rack is flush against the post and out of the way.

— *Fran Devereux Smith*
Peyton, Colorado

Halters and Hay Nets

HERE ARE TWO invitations to trouble: A dangling halter and a hay net tied too low. All too often the halter is left like this after the horse is saddled at the trailer. Before you ride off, or when you come back, the horse can easily stick a foot into it, causing a wreck. The same can happen with a hay net; it should always be tied short and high so there's no chance a horse can get a foot into it, whether it's empty or stuffed with hay.

— *Pat Close*
Elizabeth, Colorado

Storage Solutions

TO PREVENT CLUTTER in your washrack, store sponges, shampoos and other horse-bathing items in three-tiered wire hanging baskets (shown at right, available at kitchen-supply stores for about $10), hung from the ceiling. Air circulates through the baskets, quickly drying the items.

Tackle or toolboxes (shown below) are great for organizing and sorting small show necessities. Items to include: safety pins, hairnets, bobby pins, a sewing kit, accessories and cosmetics.

— Jennifer Denison
Woodland Park, Colorado

SCOTT MILLER

JENNIFER DENISON

VINTAGE — Horseman's Scrapbook

Bale Barrow

An old wheelbarrow is the basis for this hint. My drawing shows how to modify the wheelbarrow without further explanation. If you have to move a few bales of hay at a time, this is a handy way to do it.

— Randy Steffen

Build Your Own Saddle Stand

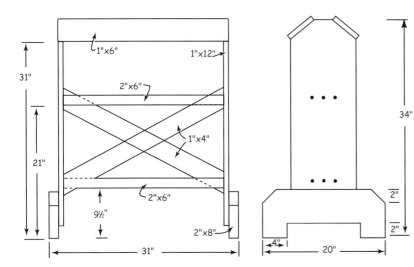

Pilot holes, countersinking and beveled edges all give the saddle stand a more finished look.

Materials Needed:
(Use grade 3 boards)
- 1 1-by-12-by-8
- 1 1-by-6-by-6
- 1 1-by-4-by-8
- 1 2-by-6-by-6
- 1 2-by-8-by-4
- 12 2¾-inch deck screws (galvanized/zinc-coated)
- 30 2-inch deck screws (galvanized/zinc-coated)
- wood glue

Tools needed:
circular saw
hand saw
electric drill
sander
screwdriver

WITH A FEW TOOLS and a little know-how, you can build a stout and attractive saddle stand in three to four hours for only $25 to $30.

Selecting wood for the project is just as important as the actual construction. Use grade 3 boards for this project. Spending the time to sort through dozens of boards to find the right ones is well worth it. When choosing the wood, check for loose knots, make sure the board isn't warped, is dried well and not heavy with moisture, and make sure any cracks don't extend into the part of the board you'll be using.

All pieces, except the cross braces, should be cut and sanded before assembly, as sanding is much easier at that point. The cross braces can be set aside and will be easier to measure once the stand is together.

Pilot holes are a must because they keep the wood from splitting when you insert the screws. A ⅛-inch drill bit works well for drilling the pilot holes. It's also a good idea to drill the holes with a countersink bit so that you can seat the screws deeper and keep them from protruding and snagging on things.

All screws should be galvanized or zinc-coated to prevent rusting. Use the 12 2¾-inch screws to fasten the 2-by-6 horizontal braces. Fasten all other pieces with 2-inch screws. The cutouts on the bottoms of the legs aren't mandatory, but will make the stand more stable on uneven ground.

The dimensions of this saddle stand seemed to work well for me. However, you may want to alter it. The way to finish the stand is up to you, whether you paint it or put a good coat of varnish on it. Just make sure all edges and corners are sanded smooth to prevent splinters and snagging.

— *Bert Anderson*
Colorado Springs, Colorado

Stall Poster

HERE'S AN INTERESTING and useful way to make posters from show photos of your horse or one of his or her relatives. Drug stores and discount chains offering photo finishing often send photos out to be made into posters at a reasonable price. Photography stores are another source.

At an art store, purchase large standard mat boards, one for each poster. These boards come in a variety of colors, with an attractive mat finish. With a grommet tool you can purchase at a drugstore, put a grommet in each corner of the board, about three inches from the corner, and about 1½ inches from the top or bottom. This makes it easy to hang the boards on an outside stall wall, and also (with wire or string), to hang additional posters under the one at the top.

Use scotch tape to attach the poster to the board. Attach the show record of the horse under the photo, punching out the information with a label maker.

— Lynda Layne
Winchester Bay, Oregon

Equipment Hanger

TO MAKE THIS HANGER, start with a simple 2-by-4, 4 to 8 feet long. Make sure the length of the board is consistent with the spacing of the wall studs (16 or 24 inches apart). You need two lag bolts for every tool you intend to hang on the rack.

To set measurements, start 3 inches from each end of the board, and work toward the center. This leaves room for the anchor bolts needed to attach the rack to the wall. The marks for lag bolts should be 2 inches apart for each tool, starting with the first bolt 3 inches from the end. The next set of marks should be 14 inches from the second mark. Continue this pattern, placing sets of marks 14 inches apart.

Predrill the holes for the lag bolts. Use a drill bit $\frac{1}{16}$-inch smaller than the lag bolts chosen (3½-by-¼-inch lag bolts are recom-

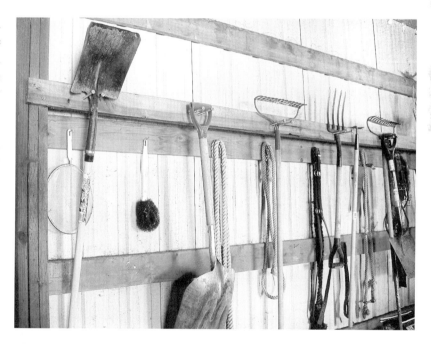

mended). Use a socket and wrench to drive the lag bolts halfway, leaving the rest of the bolt exposed.

Once all the bolts are in place, predrill holes through the 2-by-4 at points appropriate for stud measurements. Then premark the walls at the desired height, just above head level, to hang the rack. Attach the rack to the wall by placing the first anchor bolt as close to the center of the board as possible, which enables the rack to be straightened, if necessary. Install the remaining anchor bolts, and the rack is ready for use.

If the rack is for tack instead of tools, only one lag bolt is needed per item, and lag bolts can be installed at 6-inch intervals.

— Scott Miller
Peyton, Colorado

Amazing Manure Master

Step 1.

Step 2.

Step 3.

BEING CHRONICALLY LAZY, I wasn't interested in shoveling manure twice to install it into our suburban-necessity dumpster: first into the wheelbarrow and then again into the dumpster itself. Realizing the inherent gravity of the situation, I created the ManureMaster 2000.

Fabricated by my local horse trailer repair shop from 1-inch-square steel tubing, the ManureMaster 2000 hangs over the edge of a standard 3-cubic-yard dumpster and allows a removable ramp (I bought mine at a motorcycle shop) to rest on the gadget's step, so a wheelbarrow easily rolls to dumpster-lip height to deliver a load. It's fast, it's easy and it amazes the neighbors.

1. ManureMaster 2000 (white rack) fits over dumpster lip to support a ramp to deliver loaded wheelbarrows for gravity emptying.
2. The wheelbarrow tire falls into the tubing-framed box and the wheelbarrow's lip fits above the dumpster so the wheelbarrow is steadied before…
3. … the road apple flip! I'm tall enough to straddle the ramp and still up-end a loaded wheelbarrow. Someone shorter should place a broad, wide step under the ramp so they have enough leverage to achieve their flip.

The ManureMaster 2000 makes horsehold chores a breeze! It really does work great, and you can weld it in about an hour from scrap materials.

— *Suzanne Drnec*
Chino, California

Tarp Tie-Down

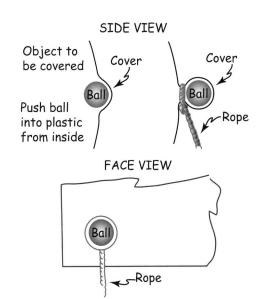

SIDE VIEW

Object to be covered

Cover

Cover

Ball

Ball

Push ball into plastic from inside

Rope

FACE VIEW

Ball

Rope

THERE ARE OCCASIONS when you need to tie a plastic or canvas tarp over a haystack to protect it from the weather, but you find that the grommets are missing or in the wrong places. You can still tie it down securely.

Pick up some inexpensive rubber balls, about the size of tennis balls (2 inches across). Place each ball under the tarp where you want it and then wrap your rope or twine around the tarp and ball a couple of times. Then use a trucker's knot and tie your rope off. If you don't want to use rubber balls, you can use old socks or anything else that's soft and has no sharp edges.

— *Dwaine Fosler*
Milford, Nebraska

Saddle Rack

HERE'S A THREE-SADDLE rack that you can mount to a tack-room wall. To make it you'll need: ½-inch channel iron (¼-inch thick) for the frame, which consists of two vertical strips with four holes in each side for mounting, plus the three 10 inch-long horizontal strips of channel iron. The three saddle racks consist of ½-inch rod, and you simply weld them to the frame.

— Randy Witte
Peyton, Colorado

Saddle Blanket Rack

HERE'S AN EASY WAY to construct a simple, two-blanket rack that can hold two 30-inch blankets. You'll need:

Back braces: two 1-by-4-by-32-inch pine boards
Side support: two 1-by-6-by-21-inch pine boards
Hangers: 1-by-34-inch round dowels (broom handles will work)
White glue
Finishing nails: size eight or six
Drill with 1-inch bit and ¼-inch bits
Paint or varnish
Brush
Sand paper
Hammer

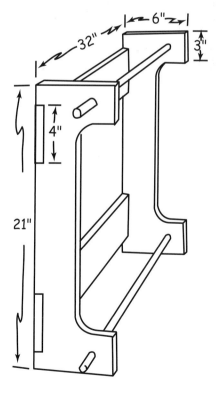

The only precision cutting required is in the side supports. In each support, cut out a 1-by-4-inch notch near the top and bottom in which to nail and glue the back supports.

Next, cut out the middle portion of the front of each support, leaving a projection, top and bottom, in which to drill holes for the dowels.

Now drill 1-inch holes for the dowels. Secure each dowel by nailing in from the top and/or bottom.

Drill ¼-inch holes in the back brace (top) in which to start the ⅜-inch screws. Screw the rack to the wall through these holes.

Sand and paint the rack before hanging.

When you hang your wet saddle blankets on this rack, they'll dry quickly and hold their shape.

— Evelyn Hicks
Sedalia, Missouri

Chalkboard Tip

WHENEVER YOU go trail riding alone, it's always best to inform someone of where you're riding and how long you'll be gone. If an accident should occur, someone will know where to look for you. Many stables hang a chalkboard on a wall inside the barn to leave messages for the farrier, veterinarian or hired help. You can also use this chalkboard to leave messages about your trail-riding activities. If no one is at the barn, write a short note to let your family or friends know you're riding. Always include the time you left, a brief description of where you're riding and the approximate return time. This is a good safety measure and might come in handy one day. You can purchase inexpensive chalkboards at office-supply stores or discount department stores. A dry-erase board may also be used.

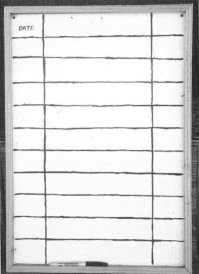

— *Martha Branon Holden*
Yadkinville, North Carolina

Peg-Board Tip

PEG BOARD has many uses in the home and it's ideally suited to the tack room because it provides a convenient way to hang a lot of gear. It can also be used for a gun rack. Make hooks from sections of aluminum rods like those used by utility companies. The rods are just the right size for a snug fit in the pegboard holes, and can be formed easily with a pair of pliers.

— *Randy Steffen*
Loomis, California

Recycled Rack

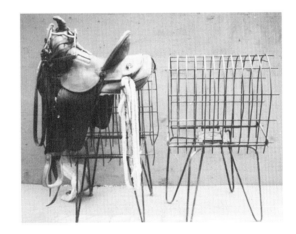

HERE'S A SADDLE RACK we've made from recycled discards—a television stand placed under a corn tunnel.

The tunnels were used in storing ear corn. Nowadays, farmers store shelled corn. My wife and mother-in-law also use the tunnels for tomato supports and such.

The saddle racks are lightweight, stable, free and portable. We find them particularly practical when oiling saddles.

— *M.E. Ehrhardt*
Mahomet, Illinois

Blanket Rack

HORSE TRAINER Gordon Brookshire of Bluff City, Tenn., has this easy-to-make and handy-to-use blanket rack installed just inside his barn door. The six-bar rack swings in, flush against the interior barn wall, should he need to close the barn door during inclement weather. Gordon can swing the rack into the barn aisle for easy access to blankets and pads when he's saddling horses, and he can even swing the rack to the outside, to air-dry wet saddle blankets more quickly in the sunshine.

He made each horizontal blanket bar and its support arm of ½-inch solid rod, first welding the support arm underneath the horizontal bar and then welding the ends of each bar and its support arm to a vertical upright.

The swing-out rack provides easy access to saddle blankets and pads.

Before welding the top wall bracket, position the L-shaped rod with the 2-inch section pointing down.

The horizontal bars are 30 inches long, sufficient to hold 34-inch saddle blankets and pads, according to Gordon, and each support arm is 6 inches long. If desired, place plastic furniture end caps over the end of each bar to keep the rod from snagging or tearing an expensive blanket.

Gordon used ¾-inch, open-ended iron pipe for his upright, making it tall enough to accommodate the six bars. However, the height of the upright pipe can vary with the desired number of blanket bars.

Horseshoes and additional ½-inch solid rod make up the top and bottom brackets for mounting the blanket rack to his barn wall. First, Gordon cut two 6-inch pieces of ½-inch solid rod, then bent each rod in a 90-degree angle 2 inches from one end. Then he welded the longer, 4-inch end of the L-shaped rod to the toe of each horseshoe. The shorter, 2-inch end is inserted into either end of the vertical pipe to hold the blanket rack upright.

The important thing, according to Gordon, is to turn each L-shaped rod in the correct direction before welding it to a horseshoe. Turn one 2-inch rod section down so it can be inserted into the top of the

For the bottom wall bracket, be sure the shorter section of the L-shaped rod points up before welding it to the shoe.

upright pipe. Turn the other 2-inch rod section up before welding for insertion in the bottom of the pipe.

To mount the blanket rack, fasten the horseshoe with the turned-up rod low on the barn wall, allowing ample clearance for the rack to swing freely above the ground. Then place the lower end of the open pipe over the vertical 2-inch rod welded to the horseshoe. Next, insert the turned-down section of the top bracket into the top of the open pipe and rotate the bracket until the horseshoe is flush with the wall. Fasten the horseshoe bracket to the wall, and your blanket rack is ready to use.

— *Fran Devereux Smith*
Peyton, Colorado

Hay-Elevator Hoist

FOR SEVEAL YEARS we struggled with the problem of storing and transporting our hay elevator. We devised a simple solution by storing our elevator overhead in the barn. The stable has a completely open 16-foot aisleway, with

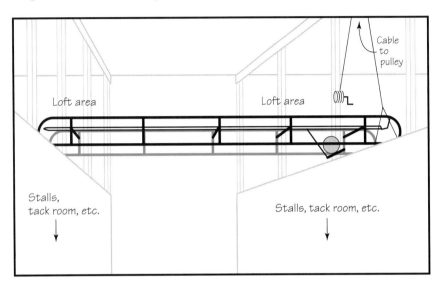

no loft directly overhead. The loft area is over each row of stalls on either side of the aisleway.

The ends of the elevator rest on the edges of the north and south lofts. We attached a cable and winch to the motorized, loading end of the elevator. This allows us to raise and lower it quickly and easily. Simply scoot back the delivery end of the elevator (it's already in the proper place in the loft), then lower the loading end to the ground by using the cable and winch, and you're ready for action.

— *Martha Branon Holden*
Yadkinville, North Carolina

Chain Hanger

HERE'S HOW TO make a handy hanger for halters, horse blankets, sweat hoods and other stable items. Take a length of lightweight chain and put a metal snap on each end. Snap the chain around something to form the hanger. For example, fasten the chain around the vertical bars on the top portion of the stall.

— *Chuck King*
Colorado Springs, Colorado

Take-Down Saddle Rack

THIS RACK HANGS from an eye-screw, and you could install a screw in your trailer, or make a bracket with a screw attached to fit over a panel at a horse show.

The 32-inch rack is made on a 6-inch piece of PVC pipe with wooden sidepieces attached with screws. The 1¼-inch D-ring that hooks to the eye-screw attached with three screws. The eye of the screw is 2 inches. A piece of plywood was screwed to the wall end of the pipe.

The PVC pipe is a handy holder for brushes and currycombs.

— *Mike Laughlin*
Eureka, Nevada

No-Roll Saddle Stand

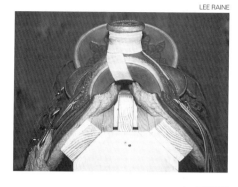
LEE RAINE

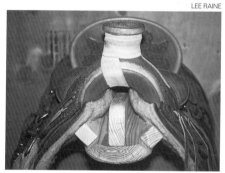
LEE RAINE

DOES YOUR SADDLE roll or tip off its saddle stand? If so, you might like this solution.

You can make the basic wooden saddle stands either of 2-by-6s, as in the free-standing tree shown in the top photo, or from shaped 2-by-8s, like the wall-mounted tree shown in the bottom photo. Add tapered and rounded wooden pieces, one on each side under the front of the bars, simulating the shoulders of a horse, and one in the center to steady the gullet of the saddle. Attach the pieces with screws. Recess the heads of the screws so they won't catch on the saddle lining.

Now your saddle will stay in place.

— *Mike Laughlin*
Eureka, Nevada

Blanket Hangers

THESE SIMPLE blanket hangers are handy to have inside your tack room. After each use you can store your saddle pad or blanket on the hanger, and it'll usually dry overnight. Another advantage is that the wet underside isn't exposed to settling dust, and the blanket stays cleaner for a longer time.

You can make these hangers as long as you like, but anything longer than 6 feet or so could start to sag under the weight of the pads. A 6-foot hanger will usually hold two pads pretty well.

You can use wooden dowels or pipe. If you choose wood, be sure to use the heavy dowels commonly used in clothes closets as hanger rods. Anything less will bow under the weight. A length of 1½-inch pipe should also work well.

Hang the rods between two 2-by-4s or 4-by-4s to keep them away from the wall enough to easily hang the blankets.

The hangers in the photo are on 4-by-4s because they were part of the structure of the room, but 2-by-4s should also work well.

A simple hook and eye is used to hang the dowels. Screw the eye into the 2-by-4 or 4-by-4 supports and the hook into each end of the dowel. Then hang the dowels from the eyes, and your blanket hanger is ready for use.

— *Rick Swan*
Scottsdale, Arizona

WATERING SYSTEMS

Horse-Proof Stock-Tank Heater

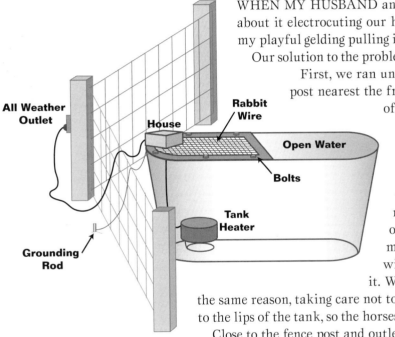

WHEN MY HUSBAND and I purchased a stock-tank heater, I worried about it electrocuting our horses when they chewed the cord, and about my playful gelding pulling it out of the tank.

Our solution to the problem was to set up a foolproof installation.

First, we ran underground wiring from the barn to the fence post nearest the frost-free hydrant. We ran wiring up the back of the fence post in steel conduit and installed a weatherproof outlet. We located the wiring and a grounding rod outside the fence.

We situated the rectangular stock tank close to the fence post with the length of the tank set at a right angle to the fence. (A round tank would also work.) We covered half of the tank with a lid. The lid can be either metal or exterior plywood. We stapled rabbit wire to the wood to prevent horses from chewing it. We also edged it with sheet-metal molding for the same reason, taking care not to leave any sharp edges. We then bolted the lid to the lips of the tank, so the horses couldn't knock it off.

Close to the fence post and outlet, we drilled a hole in the lid to accommodate the tank-heater cord. We built a three-sided "house" (also covered with rabbit wire and edged with metal molding) over the hole, with the open side facing the fence. That allowed the cord to exit directly through the fence and up the post to the outlet.

We adjusted the cord to a sufficient length that permitted the heater to sink with the water level, yet didn't allow it to float to the open end of the tank where horses could grab it. We left excess cord outside the fence. I use a short length of hose to fill the tank.

We attached a grounding wire to one of the bolts underneath the tank lip (near the fence), then connected it to the grounding rod located outside the fence.

The project of making the lid took only a few hours. The cost was minimal, and because the heater itself is protected from the elements, it should last many seasons.

— Linda J. Marshall
Boulder, Colorado

Gravity-Flow Waterer

WHAT SHOULD YOU DO when you have five water tanks to keep full and only one float? Here's how we solved that problem.

We placed the waterer with the float outside the fence and covered it to keep it clean. A drain in the bottom feeds water to the other tanks set up in tandem with interconnecting drains. Gravity takes care of the rest.

— *Richard Schroepfer*
Visalia, California

VINTAGE — Horseman's Scrapbook

Automatic Waterer

This automatic-watering device is easy to make and is useful in most any stable situation. Mount a toilet-float valve on the edge of the trough, with a garden hose attached to the feed connection. The float automatically keeps the water level constant. A simple iron-rod guard welded to the tank will keep playful horses and colts from pushing the float around with their noses.

— *Randy Steffen*

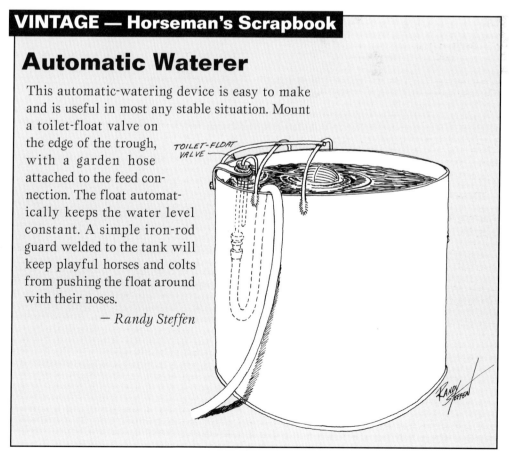

TOILET-FLOAT VALVE

Ice-Free Water Tanks

HERE'S HOW PAUL WARSICKI of the Double JJ Resort Ranch at Rothbury, Mich., keeps his water tanks free of ice on all but the coldest winter days.

Paul said he tried using tank water heaters, but wasn't satisfied with the electric bill that came each month. So now he uses submersible pumps in the tanks — the kind of pumps used to decorate waterfalls and fountains by continuously re-circulating the water. The re-circulated water doesn't freeze.

"Ray Rickard got the idea for this circulator from watching an aerator placed under a pier in a lake for environmental reasons," Paul said. "Ray noticed that the water never froze where it was bubbling."

Paul's pump, rated at 115 volts and 5 amperes, is available through most chain stores and sells for between $40 and $50. Most are guaranteed for 10,000 continuous hours. Ray's pump is modified slightly, as the diagram shows.

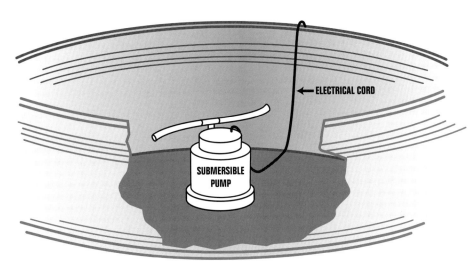

← ELECTRICAL CORD

SUBMERSIBLE PUMP

He's placed a "T" pipe on the pump's outlet so the water is forced to either side, providing better circulation.

Of course, the electrical cord should be situated so horses cannot get hold of it with their teeth.

Paul said one of his pumps keeps a 300-gallon tank ice-free down to about 15 degrees below zero, with a wind chill of about minus 40. And then only a thin film of ice forms, and it's easily broken by a horse's nose.

— WH *Editorial Staff*
Colorado Springs, Colorado

Water Wonders

YOU CAN MAKE two water tubs out of a 50-gallon, plastic barrel. Simply cut the barrel in half using a handsaw. Then thoroughly clean each half of the barrel. Finish by filling each half with fresh water. (*Tip:* If you live in a cold climate, use a black barrel. It'll warm up quickly in sunshine, thus melt ice.)

— *Jennifer Denison*
Woodland Park, Colorado

Water-Tank Floats

A BROKEN WATER TANK FLOAT is a serious problem. In addition to making a muddy mess, there's an increase in wear on the pump, a larger power bill and, in certain situations, loss of precious stored water.

The most reliable stock-tank floats I've used are made of a coffee can filled with rounds cut from 1-inch styrofoam insulation.

To make one: Mark the foam to fit tightly inside the can and push enough rounds in the can to almost fill it. Punch two small holes in the can to tie on a wire bail. It's important to use heavy galvanized or stainless wire so that the wire doesn't rust and fail before the can rusts.

Hook the float to the valve-lever rod using a brass chain with swivels and "S" hooks.

— Jack Adkins
American Falls, Idaho

Escape Route

IN SOME PARTS of the country, birds and small animals are attracted to stock tanks for water. Unless the tank is full, they can fall in and drown.

The photo shows how to save them and keep your tank from being contaminated. A plank or a fence post in the tank allows the critter to climb out. Wire the plank to the fence or the side so your horses won't bump into it.

— Wilbur Adank
Hebron, Indiana

Tank-Heater Safety Tip

HERE'S A SAFETY TIP to prevent horses from receiving a severe electrical shock due to a defective water-tank heater. Some horses can be killed by the shock, and others won't drink from a tank again and have to be watered by bucket.

You can reduce the hazards of electrical equipment around livestock and humans by using a device called a ground fault interruptor (GFI). This gadget detects the flow of electrical current from power wiring to ground. If the current is greater than the safe limit, the GFI breaks the circuit.

This device is very sensitive and responds so quickly that a severe shock is prevented before the victim can even feel it. You can purchase a GFI built into an electrical outlet, which will replace any ordinary outlet. It's available at most retail electrical supply stores.

Keeping electrical equipment in good condition is important, but a GFI will provide even greater protection against accidents.

— Richard Humphrey
San Jose, California

85

Frozen-Pipe Prevention

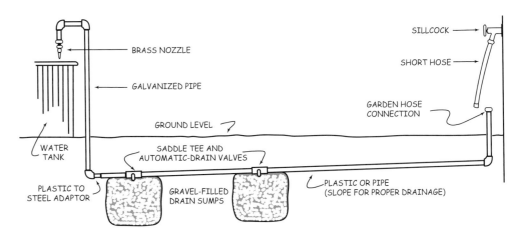

AFTER A LITTLE experimenting, I came up with this method of preventing frozen pipes. My setup isn't much different from others you've probably seen, except for one detail: I use automatic-drain valves above the sumps.

The automatic valves — and the saddle tees used to install them — are available at most hardware stores. Two valves should be sufficient, but you might want to install three just to be sure. Place one valve at the lowest point on the line.

The valves should be installed at about a 45-degree downward angle. Slip a piece of 3-inch pipe over the valves and saddle tees for protection. You might have to slit the pipe slightly in order to slide it over the valve. Dig a gravel-filled sump beneath each valve.

The only problem I had with this arrangement was insufficient pressure on the ¾-inch line. I solved this problem by putting a brass nozzle on the outlet pipe. I suggest that you check the operation of the valves before they're buried.

— *Wayne Smith*
Cheyenne, Wyoming

Easy Icebreaker

HERE'S A TRICK that I learned from my dad, who lives in the South where a frozen water trough is an occasional problem, one that seldom warrants the expense of a stock-tank heater.

He simply puts a wooden fence post a few inches in diameter in the trough, with one end sticking out of the water; a tree-limb will work, too. As the temperature drops and the water freezes, the water climbs the post, leaving a sizable air gap between the frozen surface and the water below.

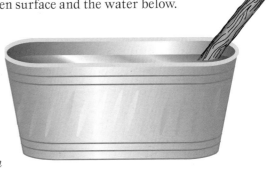

A couple of tugs on the post the next morning, and the ice breaks without splashing cold water everywhere. A stall fork works great to scoop ice from the trough.

This idea has worked fairly well for me in Colorado. Granted, my trough is under a run-in shed and protected from the northern wind, but a tank-heater isn't an option right now. Nonetheless, a 2-by-2-inch post in the trough has been a good icebreaker the past few winters.

— *Fran Devereux Smith*
Peyton, Colorado

Homemade Gravity-Flow Portable Water Tank

YOU CAN USE THIS for trail rides, tree watering or any-place where water is limited. You can easily load and fill it in a truck bed, utility vehicle or even a wheelbarrow. You'll need:

1   50-gallon plastic drum (Make sure all previous contents have been cleaned out thoroughly.)
1   3-inch long, 1-inch diameter steel pipe (threaded at both ends)
1   plastic quick-disconnect hose fitting with shut-off valve
1   section of garden hose (no less than 8 feet long)
1   2-by-4s (2 feet long)
2   4-by-4s (3 feet long)
2   4-by-4 board pieces (4 inches long and cut at 45-degree angle to create two angled blocks)
1   corrugated wooden strip, 2 feet long (used for hanging corrugated fiberglass)
12 3-inch deck screws
8   1-inch wood screws

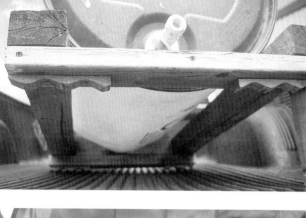

The barrel will have two screw-in type lids in the top. Drill the center out of one lid to establish a fitting for the threaded pipe. Insert the threaded pipe in the center of the drilled-out lid. Attach the quick-disconnect fitting to the outside end of the pipe. Attach the other half of the quick-disconnect fitting to the garden hose.

To create the base, start with the 2-by-4s. Using deck screws, attach one end of a 2-by-4 to the end of one 4-by-4 at a 90-degree angle. Do the same with the opposite end of the 2-by-4, leaving 4-by-4s parallel to each other. Attach the other 2-by-4 to the 4-by-4s, creating a rectangle.

Cut the corrugated strip into four equal pieces. Attach a piece of corrugated strip to each end of the 2-by-4s, ensuring that they're in line with the 2-by-4s. (Use the wood screws.)

Create angled blocks by cutting a 45-degree angle 1-inch from a piece of a 4-by-4. Measure 4½ inches from the point of the remaining piece and cut at a 90-degree angle. This should create two identical blocks.

Turn the rectangle over so that the 4-by-4s are on top. At one end of rectangle place blocks on top of the 2-by-4, thick end against each of the 4-by-4s. Attach the blocks with 3-inch deck screws. This creates a valley for the barrel to rest in.

Lay the barrel in the cradle with the solid end resting in the blocks. Make sure that the quick-disconnect fitting is at the bottom of the barrel when the barrel is laid in the cradle. This leaves the other lid at the top of the barrel for filling. Make sure you place the barrel in the proper vehicle or location prior to filling with water. The corrugated strips help stabilize the cradle in the bed of a pickup.

— *Scott Miller*
Peyton, Colorado

Water-Tank Patch

HAVE YOU EVER HAD a hole in your water tank that you couldn't repair because the nearest welder was 20 miles away? If so, here's a handy way to patch it using a ¼-by-2-inch bolt, a ¼-inch nut, two ¼-inch washers and two other larger metal washers. In addition, you'll need two more washers (homemade) made of leather or inner tube cut to an outside diameter larger than your large metal washers.

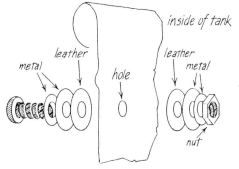

Start by placing the small (¼-inch) washer on the bolt, and then follow that with the large metal washer and the leather washer. With the washers on the bolt, place it through the hole in the tank from the outside.

Next, on the inside of the tank, over the bolt, place the leather washer, then the large metal washer and then ¼-inch washer. Now, screw on the nut and tighten securely. The hole is fixed!

I have tanks that haven't leaked for 8 years after being repaired like this.

— *Bob Johnson*
Dove Creek, Colorado

Water-Trough Clean-Up

HERE ARE TWO tips for cleaning your horse's water trough. Remove floating debris by running a kitchen strainer through the water. To remove algae or encrusted grime, first empty the trough. Then use a long-handled scrub brush to clean the tub. Rinse thoroughly and refill.

— *Jennifer Denison*
Woodland Park, Colorado

No-Spill Water Buckets

WE'VE ALL SUFFERED wet legs while toting pails of water. But if you don't fill up the buckets, you have to make more trips. Now there's a better way. Just put a plastic trash bag in the bucket, folding the top down over the rim. Fill the pail right to the top, then pull the top together, twist and tie.

The same principle works for larger containers. If you don't have a piece of plastic big enough to line the container, fill it up to about the three-quarter level, then float some clean pieces of wood in the water. This breaks up wave motion and cuts down on slosh.

— *Deborah Tompkins*
Greenville, New York

Tank Tires

HERE'S A MONEY-SAVING IDEA I've used to keep ice out of my stock tank in lieu of a tank heater.

Stack three large truck tires vertically and fill the area inside each tire with old hay or straw, leaving room in the center of the stack to insert a plastic drum. Cut the drum level with the top of the tire stack, then place the drum inside the stack and on a bed of straw. No more high-dollar electric bills.

When I started using this idea, we had a couple of 20-below-zero nights and a week with highs around zero. The only ice I had to break was about an inch thick on top. But a two-tire-high stack won't work; the water freezes.

A hint: Most trucking companies are glad to part with junk tires, because the company generally has to pay for disposal.

— *Diane Walker*
Fort Lupton, Colorado

Tank-Heater Protection

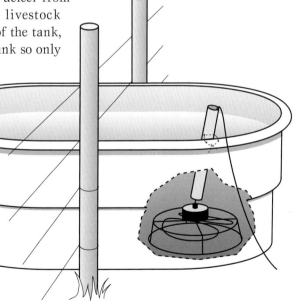

TO PROTECT OUR submersible deicer from accidental damage, such as the livestock chewing on it or flipping it out of the tank, we located our 100-gallon stock tank so only half of it is inside the fence. Our deicer is placed in the end of the tank outside the fence.

For further protection, we put a piece of PVC pipe, 29 inches long and 2 inches in diameter, over the length of the electrical cord. We drilled two holes in the upper part of the pipe and in the upper edge of the stock tank. We inserted a small piece of wire through the holes in the PVC and those in the tank. Then we twisted the wire tightly. The deicer is now firmly anchored, safe and secured to the end of the stock tank that's inaccessible to livestock.

— *Martha Branon Holden*
Yadkinville, North Carolina

PASTURE, CORRAL AND ARENA EQUIPMENT

Windbreak Shelter

ALTHOUGH I BUILT A machinery barn with a couple of stalls in it when we moved to another farm, I also had one lot with no shelter on it. So I built a windbreak with material I had on hand, except for the bolts, wood screws and roofing metal.

I built my windbreak in three 10-foot-long sections, but the size can vary depending on how many horses you want to shelter.

I cut four 5-inch diameter posts into 12-foot lengths and set them upright with one post in the center. From the outside edge of the planned roof to the center post is about 6 feet.

For each section of the windbreak, I bolted three 10-foot 1-by-6s of red oak to the posts to use as nailers. Then, using deck screws, I attached 8-foot 1-by-8s upright to the nailers.

For the roof framing, I fastened 18-foot 2-by-6s to the perimeter posts at an 8-foot height. I then ran 1-by-6s crossways and fastened galvanized roofing to them with screws. I even added guttering on the south side of the windbreak and attached a feedbox near the center post.

With this shelter, no matter which way the wind blows, an animal can find protection.

— *Robert Baker*
Hamilton, Missouri

2" x 6" roof supports
Roof edge
10' wall sections
5" diameter posts

Simple Stile

I HAVE A PASTURE that's cross-fenced with steel T-posts and woven wire, with a gate in one corner. I really didn't need another gate in the middle of the fence, but there were times when it would've been handy to cross over the fence without walking down to the gate.

So, one evening after work, I used some scrap material to build this stile — nothing fancy, but it sure works and is safe for horses. I used 6-by-6-inch timbers that had rotted off at ground level in a horse run and had to be replaced. I trimmed

them and set one timber about 3-feet deep next to the fence, then I set the other three only a few inches into the ground and nailed everything together. Then, for added strength, I bound the posts together with baling wire. I even wired an old rake handle to the T-post for a person to grab while stepping over the fence.

Most of my home projects don't turn out nearly as good as this one did.

— *Randy Witte*
Peyton, Colorado

VINTAGE — Horseman's Scrapbook

Feed Bunk

Here's a feed bunk that's weatherproof with the lid down, and a windbreak for horses or cattle with the lid up. Made of scrap lumber, it makes loading a snap from the alleyway into a set of corrals.

— *Randy Steffen*

Arena Groomer

MY HUSBAND SAVES everything, so he welded some old pipe, mesh wire and horseshoes to make a "groomer" for the arena and the round pen. He made a pipe frame and attached the mesh. Then he welded a row of horseshoes onto the frame and added a couple horseshoes on the opposite corners with a chain between them for towing the groomer.

By flipping down the curved ends of the shoes, he makes hasty work of smoothing the sand in our 50-foot round pen. He uses the groomer with the open ends of the horseshoes turned down to drag the harder dirt in our larger riding arena. Towing the groomer from the saddle horn is great for a horse; it gives him a job and a weight to drag.

— Jeannine and Butch Wright
Powell, Wyoming

The arena groomer is welded together from old pipe, mesh wire and horseshoes.

Butch Wright drags the arena.

Pole Holders

THESE EASY-TO-MAKE pole holders are handy for schooling trail horses at home and for setting up trail courses at shows. They secure poles firmly, preventing them from rolling should a horse tick them. At home when you're schooling, this eliminates dismounting and resetting a pole every time your horse rolls one.

In the past, I always schooled young horses on railroad ties or telephone poles. To convince him that if he bumped it, he couldn't move it, so he'd better be careful. Now, I derive the same benefits from using jump poles with the holders.

Our poles are made from 4-by-4-inch posts with the edges removed so they're octagonal. Set in the holders, they're immovable enough to convince a horse to pick up his feet, and they're much lighter to move than railroad ties.

Make the holders with scrap lumber, using pieces of 2-by-6-inch planks and plywood. Use a jigsaw for correct cutting of the plywood sides.

Start the basic frame with a 2-foot-long piece of 2-by-6. Then, add two upright pieces of the same type of lumber, standing 6 inches high. Before nailing them, draw a line to determine the center of the 2-foot length. Then, draw a line 2 inches to the left of the center line, and another one 2 inches to the right. This gives you a 4-inch opening. Place the "inside" of each upright piece of 2-by-6 on the lines next to the center line. Then nail or screw the upright pieces from underneath.

To make the sides, start with a piece of plywood that's a minimum of 2 feet long and 8 inches high (for each side). Lay the frame on its side on the plywood. Draw lines to indicate how the plywood should be cut. Cut the plywood shape with a jigsaw. Nail to the side of the frame with small nails to avoid splitting the plywood.

The combinations of obstacles you can put together with the pole holders are endless. Besides the normal walkovers, you can use them to secure pole ends for straight back-throughs, or L back-throughs. You can stack them for jumps. You can make a "star" by putting one pole out of each end, and let the ends of two poles share the center opening. It makes a four-corner star for walking in a circle or trotting over.

Because they're small and easily stacked, the holders make excellent portable obstacles to take with you to shows for schooling.

Since the holders lay on the ground most of the time, two coats of a high gloss paint not only make them attractive, but also protect them from excess moisture.

— *Lynda Layne*
Winchester Bay, Oregon

4-foot poles secured by the holders.

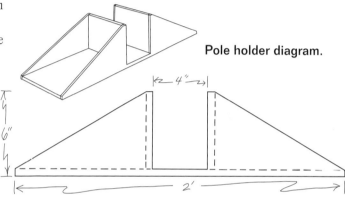

Pole holder diagram.

Trail-horse trainers will find these holders a great convenience.

Pole holders being used for an L back-through.

Hay Feeder

THESE feeders accommodate four horses. Each feeder holds a two-wire, 80-pound alfalfa bale. Feeders are heavy so horses, and especially mules, can't push them around, but light enough that you can pull them with a truck, saddle horse or four-wheeler.

The 2-by-4-inch lip keeps hay from spilling, which is especially important in sandy regions. Sand colic is possible when you feed stock on the ground.

— *R.J. Duykaerts*
Independence, California

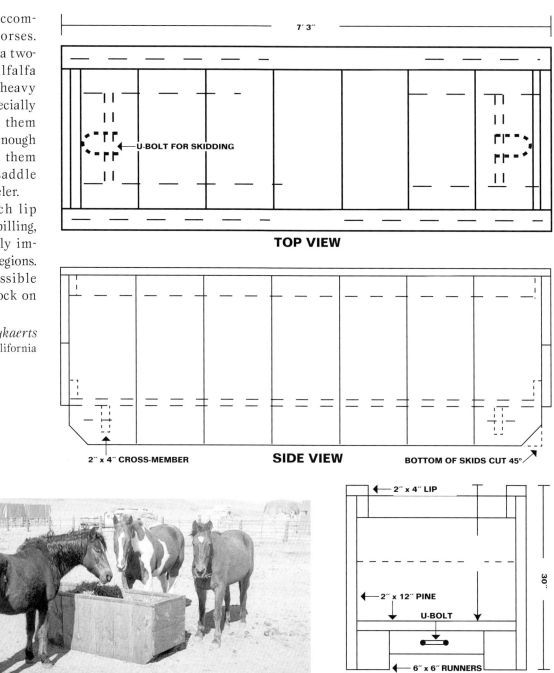

7´ 3˝

U-BOLT FOR SKIDDING

TOP VIEW

SIDE VIEW

2˝ x 4˝ CROSS-MEMBER

BOTTOM OF SKIDS CUT 45°

2˝ x 4˝ LIP

2˝ x 12˝ PINE

U-BOLT

6˝ x 6˝ RUNNERS

30˝

31˝

END

Railroad-Tie Roping Dummy

HERE'S AN EASY way to make a roping-dummy body for heading. Saw off the ends of a railroad tie and place under the remainder of the tie for legs. Nail the ends to the tie to keep them in place. Attach a practice steer head, the molded type available at most saddle shops and western stores, to one end of the tie by drilling holes in the tie. Then insert the prongs (on the head designed to shove into a bale of hay) into the holes.

— *Chuck King*
Colorado Springs, Colorado

Inexpensive Jumps

AS A RIDING INSTRUCTOR, I have students who want to try a variety of equine activities, including jumping. However, jump standards and accessories are expensive, and very few students continue jumping. But I've discovered an inexpensive way to let them test their skills.

Using 1½-inch PVC pipe, tees and elbows found in any hardware store, you can construct jumps of your own. Always use a full 10-foot length for the crossbar. I like my uprights to accommodate the crossbar in ½-foot increments — 1 foot, 1½ feet and 2 feet. You can use either PVC elbows or tees on top of the upright to attach the crossbar.

At the base of each upright, use one tee, which rests on the ground. If you prefer, use the additional upright sections (not being used to hold the crossbar) as stabilizers by attaching them to the tee on the ground. Or simply purchase enough additional PVC to leave two sections attached to each upright at ground level to help stabilize the jump.

I use an elbow on top of each upright to attach the 10-foot crossbar, but if your horse tends to duck around jumps, use a tee in the upright instead. That way, you can attach the crossbar and a longer 3- or 4-foot extension to the upright to help keep the horse on track.

You'll need:
all PVC and couplings 1½ inches in diameter
one 10-foot-long section for crossbar
two elbows for attaching crossbar
two tees for uprights
two 1-foot sections for uprights
two 1½-foot sections for uprights or use as stabilizers
two 2-foot sections for uprights or use as stabilizers

for optional upright extensions
four tees
two 3- or 4-foot sections for upright extensions
two optional end caps for extensions

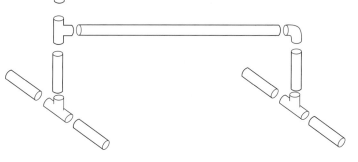

An important note: Don't glue any components into place. This jump is intended to fall apart completely if a horse hits it, minimizing the potential injury to horse and/or rider. The PVC is strong enough to resist shattering.

You can build many jump variations using PVC components; simply think of the parts as a giant jigsaw puzzle. You can use larger sizes of pipe. However, the 1½-inch diameter is adequate and costs less.

— *Stephanie Thorne*
Vermontville, Michigan

An Inexpensive Windbreak

THIS UNUSUAL windbreak isn't fancy, but it works and livestock really appreciate it when the winter winds howl.

Although the windbreak took a little time to construct, it certainly didn't cost very much — old tires are plentiful and usually free. The tires on the bottom row were threaded onto a steel pipe, and those on the top two rows are hung on cable. Although this windbreak is three spans wide, it can be made longer or shorter.

— Pat Close
Elizabeth, Colorado

Maintenance-Free Walker

THIS MAINTENANCE-FREE, two-horse walker suits the needs of many trainers and horse owners. It's safe, efficient and easy to make. Best of all, it's economical because you use materials from a junkyard.

The walker is made of steel pipe, and a wheel axle and hub. It stands 9 feet tall, with an additional 3 feet set in concrete in the ground. It measures 8 feet across at the top.

The base is similar to a Lynco axle, and it's mounted into a steel pipe. The hub on top is welded to the axle. The hub rotates on its own. The top arm is a $1\frac{7}{16}$-inch solid steel shaft, mounted on a 2-inch center brace. This top arm is welded to the hub's rim. A steel loop is welded to each end of the arm, and a chain is attached to the loop.

The walker accommodates one or two horses, and it's powered by the horses.

— Helena Hill
Hart, Texas

Portable Corral

16' Galvanized Stock Combo Rod Panel

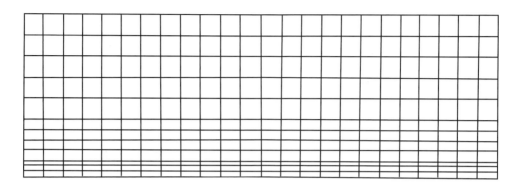

Cut Panel into Thirds

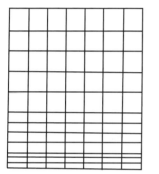
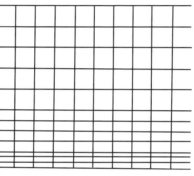

Tri-Fold Panel

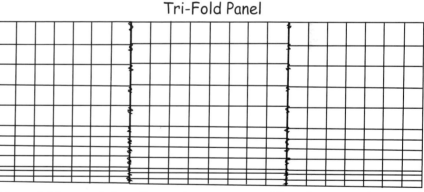

This portable corral gives the maximum amount of length, yet can be stored in a very compact area for traveling.

You'll need:

4-foot by 4½-inch by 16-foot galvanized rod-stock combination panel, sometimes referred to as a "hog panel." Panels that are welded first, and then galvanized last longer.

Steel T-posts as needed

Side view of top hinge

Arial view of top hinge

TO MAKE a handy portable corral, cut stock panels into thirds. Use the cut horizontal rods as hinges by wrapping them around the two vertical end rods of each section (see drawings). Each completed panel should measure 14 feet, 9 inches in length. This makes a tri-fold panel that's durable and inexpensive. To set up the corral, simply mount panels on steel T-posts that are driven into the ground. Make sure the panels are mounted high enough that horses can't reach over the top to graze.

— *Dwaine Fosler*
Milford, Nebraska

11 FENCING AND GATES

Barbed-Wire Spool Carrier

MY HUSBAND, Al Stohlman, showed me this barbed-wire spool carrier and demonstrated how it worked.

The carrier handles most of the weight of the spool of wire. You simply pull it along the ground. The bent ends on the bottom of the side pieces give little resistance.

The loose joints of the pipe elbows (at the hand bar) allow the carrier to ride over rocks, logs and bushes without distorting the position of the hand bar. This causes less strain on the hand and wrist.

When fencing our property in Canada, we used this carrier exclusively. Al started at the top of a hill and trotted all the way down, along the fence posts. Walking back up the hill for another spool of wire, the carrier becomes a useful tool to prop yourself against while catching your breath.

The accompanying drawings show all the parts required and their dimensions. Extra shims might be needed if the spool of wire is too loose when the unit is assembled.

— *Ann Stohlman*
Cache Creek, British Columbia

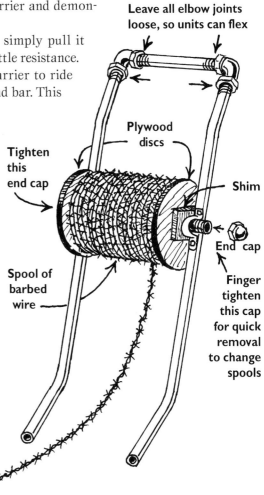

Leave all elbow joints loose, so units can flex

Plywood discs

Tighten this end cap

Shim

End cap

Finger tighten this cap for quick removal to change spools

Spool of barbed wire

Wood-Chewing Deterrent

MANY HORSES CHEW WOOD, especially when confined to small areas. In a pen or corral, where you don't want to use an electric wire to keep them away from the fencing, nor paint-on a wood preservative that might be toxic if a horse does chew, you can cover the poles or boards with chicken wire.

Small-mesh chicken wire fitted snugly over the poles or boards is one of the safest and most foolproof ways to keep a horse from chewing. Cut the chicken wire to the

proper width (with tin snips) to fit the surface you're covering, then bend under the cut ends to eliminate sharp, protruding surfaces. Staple the chicken wire to the wood at frequent intervals to keep a smooth surface. Use relatively large staples that won't pull out. The unpleasant feel of the chicken wire on the horse's teeth prevents him from chewing wood.

— *Heather Smith Thomas*
Salmon, Idaho

VINTAGE—Horseman's Scrapbook

Picket-Pole Corral

The old Southwestern picket-pole corral is a picturesque part of the great cow country; and for folks who'd like to have one on your place, the drawings show how very simple they are to make. You'll need enough 2-inch mesquite, cedar, oak or most any kind of poles, crooked or otherwise, long enough to stand up as high or as low as you want and baling wire. Set fairly stout posts every 8 to 10 feet to support the lighter picket fence. Be sure you tie the fence to these posts, top and bottom, with more baling wire. This kind of fence, while extremely rough, presents a rustic and pleasing appearance around the horse lot.

— *Randy Steffen*

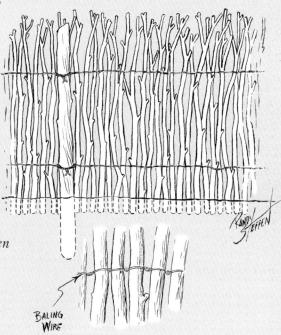

BALING WIRE

Weighted Gate

A COMMON SIGHT, in years past, was a counterbalance to shut a gate. Most gates these days have springs.

You can make the weighted gate closer out of whatever is handy, and adjust it to just exactly the right tension.

Here's how to apply this idea to your gate.

Attach a small pulley to the gate post, and run a piece of ¼-inch cotton rope through it. Attach one end to the gate. Hook the other end to a weight.

A weight that's too heavy will slam your gate too hard, and one that's not heavy enough will allow it to blow in the wind. Adjust the ballast by using a bucket of sand, and add sand until you're satisfied.

Use horseshoes as an alternative. Simply add the shoes to a loop in the end of the rope, until you have enough weight. You can use almost anything for a weight, even an old singletree or a bucket of scrap iron.

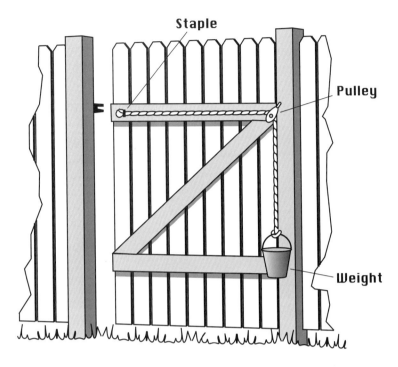

Attach the rope to the gate with staples or nails and, if needed, substitute a ring for the pulley.

To complete the gate, use a self-locking latch, so that the gate latches when shut.

— Gary Kirchmeier
Cave Creek, Arizona

Seat-Belt Gate Latch

OLD SEAT BELTS cost very little at an auto-salvage yard and can be adapted to many uses around the barn. The seat-belt latches are made of quality materials and, because the button must be pressed to open the latch, they're animal-proof. This latch was welded onto a metal strap, which was then bolted to the gate and post to make a secure gate latch.

— Fergus Rodine
Kelowna, British Columbia

Gate Safety

Figure 1.   Figure 2.

THE PLACEMENT OF THE upper hinge of a pin, pipe or tube-type gate can be critical in a horse operation. Commonly, the pin is set low, at least halfway down between the upper horizontal pipes, as shown in Figure 1.

My shoer told me he lost a good horse when the horse reared up and caught a front leg and hoof between the gate and the gate post. You can minimize this hazard by placing the upper hinge pin as high as possible on the gate post (Figure 2).

— Stan Tixier
Eden, Utah

Wire Spool

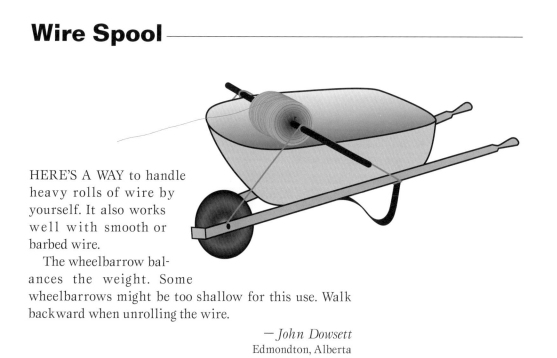

HERE'S A WAY to handle heavy rolls of wire by yourself. It also works well with smooth or barbed wire.

The wheelbarrow balances the weight. Some wheelbarrows might be too shallow for this use. Walk backward when unrolling the wire.

— John Dowsett
Edmondton, Alberta

Fencing Bag

THE TOP OF AN old cowboy boot makes a fencing bag that's been popular with ranchers for many years. To make the bag, cut the top of the boot from the foot, just above the instep. Then lace the bottom of the boot top with a leather thong. The bag has room for a fence tool, staples and hammer.

Caution: Tie the bottom of the bag with a saddle string to keep it from flopping after you slip the leather loop at top over the saddle horn for carrying.

— Chuck King
Colorado Springs, Colorado

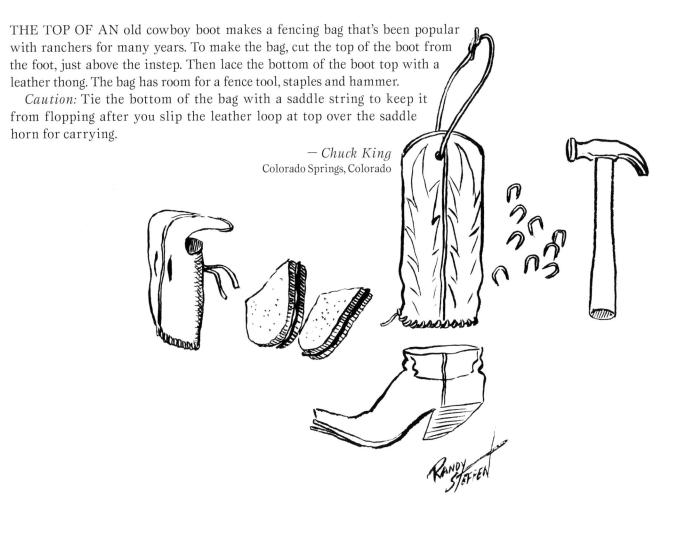

Tires for Corner Posts

SOMETIMES YOU NEED a corner post in a spot where you can't dig a hole. Here's an idea that might solve your problem.

Stack four truck or tractor tires, one on top of the other, where the corner post needs to be and fill the tires with loose rock. You can then run a strand of wire around each tire, centering the wire on the tread, before tightening the wires.

Or you can center a fence post inside the first tire and then pack rock around the post. Lay the bottom strand of fencing on top of the first tire before stacking a second tire on top and packing it. Likewise, lay another strand on top of the second tire before stacking the third, and so forth, until the corner post height suits you. With this method, the wires are pulled between the tires and snug against the post as you tighten them.

— Bill Petry
Oroville, Washington

Wretched Wire Gates

Susan Marxer of the Matador Cattle Co. in Dillon, Mont., outsmarts a tight wire gate. She doesn't advise dropping the reins in this situation, but describes the horse shown as an "honest and seasoned" ranch horse.

AS NECESSARY AS IT MIGHT BE, wire and I just don't get along. Rusty barbed wire from old homesteads lurks in the grass and sagebrush, waiting to reach out and grab my horse as I blindly trot through it. Newfangled electric wires, singing and glinting in the sun, look like snakes to my horse, who's apparently had a memorable experience with the deceptively simple barriers. I've faced a good many of the wrecks and obstacles while trying to be my husband's right hand. I owe them to that wretched wire.

The wire that gives me the most fits, though, has to be gates. Actually, I call them "Ray-gates," and "me-gates."

The distinction: Me-gates have a bit of slack in the wire, allowing me to open and close them. Ray-gates, on the other hand, are virtually impossible for me — even with a so-called cheater. When I do manage to get one open, it immediately shrinks about a foot, unless I just hook the top wire, or happen to have a piece of baling twine handy. However, my husband insists such methods are just as useless as leaving it open. So I tell him he'll just have to close it himself — which he does without so much as a grunt. Of course, if he has to backtrack me, or several hours pass before he can get to it, that can strain a relationship.

Have your horse close enough to the gate so that you can reach your saddle horn without stretching too far. Place the gate stick in the bottom wire loop of the gate post as usual. Take the loop of your rope and put it around the tops of the gate post and the gate stick, with the honda positioned so that the rope comes back at a sharp angle. Drop your coils on the ground. Be sure they won't be around your feet.

Run the rope from the gate post to your saddle horn; your back cinch should be snug. For safety's sake, don't take a full wrap; instead go around your horn and hold the rope to keep it tight. Slowly ease your horse back until you can get the top wire loop over the gate stick. That's all there is to it. No tears in your clothes, no slivers and no frustration.

Some horses get a little spooky when they realize they're hooked on to a fence. If you're not sure how your horse will react, keep control of your reins. The horse in the photos is about as honest and seasoned as a ranch horse comes; I don't turn my reins loose on just any horse.

— Susan Marxer
Dillon, Montana

103

Stout Gate Latch

THE MAN WHO BUILT this gate latch obviously has spent some time around livestock. It's stout and very secure.

The main rod is built from the power-take-off shaft off an old tractor; therefore, it's solid all the way through and extremely durable. The handle is simply a stout bolt welded into place.

What makes the latch so secure is the piece of rod welded onto the end of the PTO shaft, where it slides into the post. This "catch" is about ¾-inch long. When the handle is perpendicular to the gate, as it'd be when opening or

closing the gate, the catch faces upward, allowing the rod to slide in and out of the rectangular hole in the post. However, when you insert the rod into the post and push down on the handle, the catch prevents the rod from sliding out of the post.

— Charlie Carrel
Sheridan, Wyoming

Low-Cost Gate Hinge

WE RECEIVED TWO versions of a good gate hinge at a minimal cost. Both are built from a leaf spring off an old half-ton Ford. Hinges can be built from the leaf springs of trucks or compact cars, depending on the size of the gate you plan to hang. The eye of the spring even has a rubber bushing. The bolts used to secure the spring leaf to the 2-by-6 are cylinder head bolts from the same old Ford. The hinges can swing from a round iron peg, which can be salvaged from a discarded telephone pole or joined together with a large bolt.

— Fergus Rodine
British Columbia

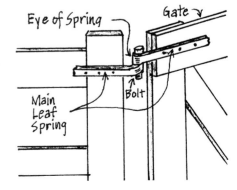

Safe-Panel Gates

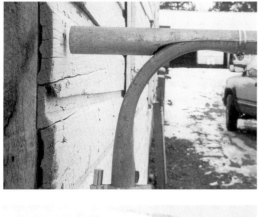

I'VE SEEN WHAT HAPPENS when a horse gets a front foot caught between two round-cornered panels. Here's what I did to my round-cornered gates to make them safe. The solution shown in the photos is simple and inexpensive. It also gives more support to light gates.

— *Dean Gumm*
Tekoa, Washington

Safer Fence

HORSES IN the Netherlands are commonly kept in barbed-wire fenced pastures. Yet when I was there last year I saw few wire-cut scars. This kind of fence post, made of steel or concrete, is the answer. It keeps the horse away from the fence, lessening the probability of a leg being caught in the wire.

If barbed wire must be used for a horse fence, this fence seems a lot safer than most. The height of these Dutch fences is about 5 feet; they often use six strands of wire, and the wire is never slack.

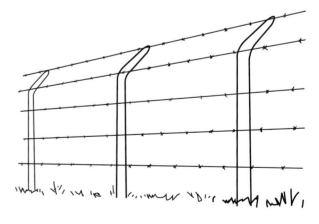

— *Robert M. Miller, D.V.M.*
Thousand Oaks, California

Gate Wheel

The 18-foot gate with the rubber lawn mower tire.

MOVING LARGE numbers of cattle or horses in and out of corrals sometimes requires a large gate opening to prevent these animals from injuring themselves or tearing down the gateposts.

At one of our horse camps, we have a water trap coming into the main set of corrals that has an 18-foot gate. This length of gate is hard on brace posts. Therefore, we've attached a rubber lawn mower tire to the bottom of the gate by using welds and frame. This gate opens and closes by rolling on the rubber tire, which supports the weight, thus preventing the gate from sagging. An 18-foot gate constructed in this manner also can be opened or closed from horseback.

— *Mike Laughlin*
Eureka, Nevada

Simple Gate Latch

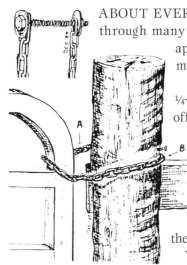

ABOUT EVERY HORSE outfit has at least one gate that you go through many times a day. I build things with the keep-it-simple approach, and this quick and handy gate latch has saved me lots of time.

The latch includes a piece of light chain joined by a ¼-inch bolt with washers to keep the chain from sliding off. The chain forms a loop that slides over the post. The key to this: If you grab the chain at Point A (much as if a horse were rubbing his head on it), the chain catches and won't slip over the post. However, if you grab it at Point B, it slides up with only one hand. The nail is optional, but serves as an effective safety latch — place it on the backside of the post so you won't snag it as you pass by.

There are many other ways to join two pieces of chain, but using a 4- or 5-inch bolt allows for some adjustment.

— *Don Straight*
Webster City, Iowa

Horseshoe Gate Latch

HERE'S A SKETCH of a gate latch that my dad, Fred Wass, developed. He's made them for many years, and I've never seen anyone else use this idea.

The latch is easy to make. You'll need an old barn-door hinge and a horseshoe. Trim one end of the hinge to fit the shoe and weld the two together.

Caution: Because this latch is larger than most, it snags things easily, and therefore should only be used on wide gates. Secondly, because this latch is easy for a horse to flip up with his nose, it isn't a secure latch for livestock gates unless a chain and snap are also used.

— *Forrest Wass*
Mariposa, California

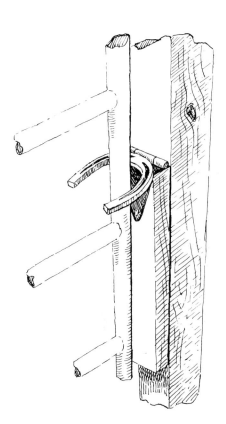

Electric-Fence Charger Cover

MOST ELECTRIC fence chargers require protection from bad weather. This usually means placing the box in the barn or under a shed. However, this isn't always an option.

Here's one way to provide shelter for your charger and still be able to view it to make sure it's working properly. Construct a three-sided box from ¾-inch plywood, waterproofed and painted to protect it from the rain. Our box is 12 inches long, 17 inches wide and 15 inches high. However, you might need to customize your box to completely cover your charger.

Nail another piece of plywood on top of the box, and cover it with galvanized metal cut to the proper size. Then attach a handle to the top to allow easy handling of the cover. On the front, screw a piece of plexiglass into the sides of the wooden box. Apply caulking around the seam between the plexiglass and wood to further weatherproof the box.

The plexiglass enables you to view the charger's light from a considerable distance. On our farm, we located the electric fence charger at a point where it can be easily seen and routinely monitored from our house.

— *Martha Branon Holden*
Yadkinville, North Carolina

Gate Bolts

TUBULAR STEEL GATES are popular among horse people because they're pre-made, come in a selection of sizes and are easy to hang. But folks often mount them wrong, as shown in the photo on the far left.

Each gate has two gate-hanger bolts that screw into the fence post. The proper way to hang the gate is to have the top bolt facing downward and the bottom bolt facing upward, as shown in the photo at left. There's a reason for this. It prevents the gate from being lifted off the bolts. Horses have been known to stick their heads through the gate braces and lift the gate off its hinges. A terrible wreck ensues because the horse thinks a monster is around his neck.

It's also best to have gates with the braces or crosspieces spaced close to one another, so a horse can't get his head stuck through them in the first place. But often this isn't the case. Therefore, the next best option is to secure the gate to the post, so the horse can't lift it. And if a gate is chained and locked, it also prevents a thief from lifting it off.

— *Kathy Swan*
Scottsdale, Arizona

Post-Puller

AFTER I THOUGHT I'd seen it all, a man showed me an easy way to get T-posts out of the ground.

Most of us have seen or used a post-pounder made of about 30 inches of 2-inch pipe closed at one end with attached handles. This same tool can help remove posts.

Put the closed end of it on the ground next to the post. Move the bottom out a couple of inches until the open top end is just under one of the metal nodes on the T-post. Put your foot against the bottom of the pounder to hold it in place, and pull the post back against it.

When you pull back, the force is converted to an upward pull, and the post will come right up. The leverage and angle are hard to describe, but after a couple of tries, you learn just the right angle. I taught this to a friend's wife and she pulled 23 posts in about 30 minutes.

— *John S. Conrad*
Sevierville, Tennessee

Horseshoe Gate-Latch Attachment

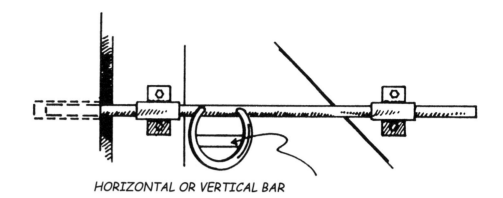

HORIZONTAL OR VERTICAL BAR

RANCHERS AND HORSEMEN have discovered an almost infinite number of uses for horseshoes — new or used — and they can be found on everything from bootjacks to living-room lamps. Weld a horseshoe to a sliding metal bar, and you've got a handy gate latch.

But there's an important attachment to the horseshoe gate latch that some do-it-yourselfers omit, and the oversight could prove costly. What's needed is a metal bar welded across the horseshoe. A curious horse can start mouthing an unaltered horse-shoe and get his lower jaw trapped in the shoe, resulting in a broken jaw. With the bar blocking the opening, a horse can't get hurt and a horseman can still use the shoe to open the gate.

— WH *Editorial Staff*
Colorado Springs, Colorado

Corral-Gate Common Sense

ANY GATE LEFT OPEN for horses, such as this corral gate into a pasture, should hang so you can secure it flush against the fence. Partially open gates can cause injuries because horses are apt to crash into them, especially if several horses are loose together and start running and playing. Hanging a gate on the outside of the post (see arrow) allows it to be opened all the way. As another safety measure, store open-wire gates standing up, not on the ground.

— *Pat Close*
Elizabeth, Colorado

12 ODDS AND ENDS

Hay Bags

ALTHOUGH THE newer hay bags, made similar to feedbags, are convenient to use and less likely to get a horse hung up, many of us still use the expandable fishnet-type hay bag. And, many of us have had a horse get a front foot caught in it. The bag, which expands horizontally when filled with hay, drops down vertically as the horse eats. As a result, the netting becomes a potential trap for the horse if not tied high enough.

SCOTT MILLER

Here's one way to help minimize a hay-bag problem. After the bag is filled, pull the top drawstring tight, and tie it in an overhand knot to keep the hay from spilling out. Then, run the tail of the drawstring through the bottom ring used as the base for the woven netting. Again, tighten the drawstring, doubling the bottom of the bag up toward the top. Tie another overhand knot here, then fasten the hay bag to your trailer.

As the horse eats, the bag still drops vertically, but it won't drop as far down, near the ground and the horse's front feet, and your horse can still reach his hay. Nothing is foolproof where a horse and a hay bag are concerned, but this might help minimize the risk.

— *Fran Devereux Smith*
Peyton, Colorado

Cold-Weather Tip

ON COLD, WINDY DAYS when you're wearing short-cuff or roper's gloves, cut the foot out of an old pair of warm socks and pull them on as wrist bands. They'll prevent the breeze from blowing up your sleeves, and they'll warm your wrists.

— *Myr Morrow*
Orangeville, Ontario

Skillet Sweetener

NEW CAST-IRON skillets, as well as Dutch ovens, sometimes give a metal flavor to foods prepared in them. Like so many people, I'd season a new skillet by rubbing it with cooking oil and heating it over a low flame. Despite that, everything I cooked tasted like metal.

But now I use another method. It's unconventional, but really works well. I fill the skillet with water and boil a handful of hay (dry hay is best) — either alfalfa or grass mix — for about 20 minutes at a rolling boil. You can use this already boiled hay water to sweeten wood and tin dishes, too. Soak them for at least 20 minutes.

— Harold Nelson
Estes Park, Colorado

Miner's Lamp

AT NIGHT, when you need both hands and some light to help you around the stable or away from home, attach a miner's lamp to your forehead. It gives off just enough light to help you watch where you're going, and it lights up the cinch when you're saddling in the dark.

— W.W. Adank
Hebron, Indiana

VINTAGE—Horseman's Scrapbook

Napkin Holder

Here's how to make a napkin holder from an old stirrup. The stirrup has the bolt and wooden spreader removed, and has been sanded down well and given a few coats of varnish. Treated this way, it makes a mighty attractive addition to the table setting in a cowboy household.

— Randy Steffen

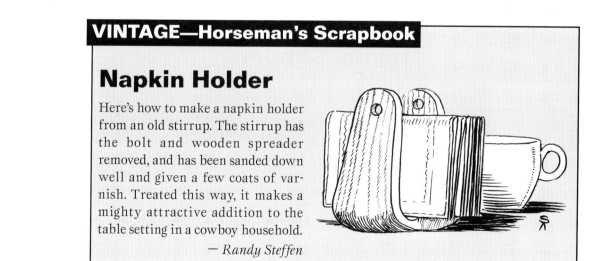

Tying Broken Bales

HERE'S HOW TO handle those untidy broken bales and secure a partially used bale, which you have to deal with when you spend a lot of time going down the road. After cutting the strings and feeding the amount of hay you need, use this handy method to retie the bale and keep the hay from blowing around in the back of your pickup.

Starting at one end of the bale, tie the end of the two strings together with a square knot.

Now run the two loose strings from the other end of the bale under and through the loop you've created. Threading the strings through the loop creates a pulley, enabling you to pull the loose bale tightly together.

Once you pull the strings nice and snug, tie an overhand loop, or slip-knot, to secure the bale. The bale is now tight enough for you to pick up and carry. You can also pull the loose ends to untie it, feed another flake and retie it in a snap.

— Charlie Carrel
Sheridan, Wyoming

Handy Clipper

WE ALL DREAD the possibility of having to go into an enclosed place to free a thrashing or hung-up horse. A large pocket knife takes two hands to open, and there's a chance of you and the horse getting cut or stabbed.

So, I keep a straight-jaw hedge clipper handy. This can be used with one hand, and will cut leather or nylon halters, or up to ¾-inch rope with one snip. The clipper, ½-inch thick and 8 inches long, fits in a pocket.

— James J. Carucio
Marengo, Illinois

Back-to-Basics Currycomb

THE BACK-TO-BASICS trend of the 1990s has invaded my tack room. An early spring and longhaired horses brought out the need for a tool to handle hair and mud that newfangled currycombs couldn't deal with.

Most kids have discarded those old, spring-loaded metal currycombs because they're too harsh. But, most people under 30 don't realize those combs have two "speeds." One side has short teeth for short hair, and the other has longer teeth for longer hair and those pesky mud-balls.

To turn the blades over, grab the handle with one hand and the blades with the other and pull — hard! As the spring gives way, simply rotate the blades. The old tool, with a little elbow grease, will have old Paint shiny in no time.

— *Don Straight*
DeSoto, Iowa

Trophy Display

HERE'S A GREAT way to display your heirloom or trophy spurs and Grandad's old rifle or bridle at the same time. For each spur, weld a slotted plate to a horseshoe, and slip the spur button into the slot. One spur strap can be left on and the spurs aren't damaged by the mounting. Use horseshoe nails to attach the shoe to your wall or a display board.

— *Jan Guelff*
Seeley Lake, Montana

Silver Polishing

GERMAN SILVER is more practical than sterling for show saddles, halters and bridles because it won't tarnish the way sterling does. But, there's still a lot of nice sterling around, and some people refer to it as German silver.

An easy way to polish silver-mounted horse gear (and belt buckles) is to scrub the metal with a soft toothbrush and toothpaste. Use a little water — just like you're brushing your teeth — then rinse. You'll get a nice fast shine.

— *Tim Haley*
Colorado Springs, Colorado

Heel Dally on Big, Fast-Movin' Steers

I ALWAYS HAD a hard time getting a heel dally on big, fast-moving steers and letting the rope go through my hand. I came up with a training aid that was inexpensive and worked well.

Cut a tractor inner tube into one strip, about 20 feet long. Tie one end to a fence post, and the other end to the honda of an old rope. Next, stretch out the rubber strip so that it has some tension in it, and mark that distance with a stake. The honda of the rope fits nicely over the top of the stake and holds it in position. Place a barrel with a saddle on top of it on the ground, a few feet past the stake.

Sit in the saddle and lift the rope, like you would for a heel catch, and pull the rope off the stake. The inner tube takes the rope away from you, giving you a good feel for the rope going through your hand on the dally. This practice really quickens your dally, too.

— *Tom Swen*
Wautoma, Wisconsin

I attach the honda of my rope to the inner tube, then hook it to a stake in the ground.

When I lift the rope, the inner tube takes the rope away from me, just as a heel loop on a fast-moving steer would.

Towel Rack

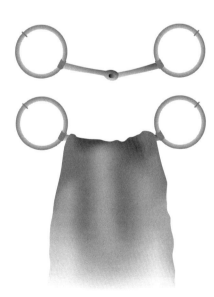

IF YOU NEED a rack for your hand towels, here's an idea that works well and will also dress up your kitchen or bathroom. An old snaffle bit works the best. Simply fasten it to the wall by driving a small utility staple over each ring. Position the rings so that there's still a little give in the mouthpiece when you're finished. That way a bulky towel can fit easily behind it.

— *Charlie Carrel*
Sheridan, Wyoming

Boot Tops

MANY COWBOYS and cattlemen are conservative by nature and by necessity. Since I had several pairs of worn-out western boots in my closet, I came up with an idea to use them.

I separated the top of the boot from the foot portion. I then shaped half the boot top to form a case for my favorite hunting knife and had my local shoe-repair shop sew it together.

The stitched pattern on the top added a nice touch to my knife case, and the same idea will work to make cases for various hand tools or a pistol.

— Dan Hayes
Kingwood, West Virginia

Recycled Film Containers

DON'T THROW AWAY those plastic 35-millimeter film containers. They're quite useful in many ways. They can hold odds and ends on long or short hauls away from home — horseshoe nails, wooden matches, coins, etc. Store these lightweight, waterproof containers in shirt pockets, saddlebags and glove compartments.

I especially like to use them for storing the correct daily dosage of crushed medicines. After crushing the pills, I pour each daily dose into a separate container. This saves time and is convenient because I have the exact dosage on hand and can leave big, cumbersome medicine bottles behind.

— Howard Guralnick
Tucson, Arizona

Color-Coded Utility Knives

SCOTT MILLER

IT'S EASY TO misplace utility knives in the barn, shop and other places after you use them. The solution is to have different colored utility knives for each area. For example, use hot pink utility knives in the barn. If you lay down the knife or carry it away, you can easily identify it as the barn utility knife, and put it back where it belongs. Utility knives come in a variety of colors and are inexpensive. Buy a different color for the barn, shop, garage and even the house.

— Karan Miller
Peyton, Colorado

Super Scoop

YOU CAN MAKE feed scoops out of empty 1-gallon milk, juice or detergent containers. First, thoroughly clean and rinse the container. Then, using a sharp knife, cut diagonally from below the handle to the container's base. Smooth any sharp edges with a metal file.

— *Jennifer Denison*
Woodland Park, Colorado

SCOTT MILLER

Leather Punch

IF YOU NEED an inexpensive leather punch, a .30-caliber bullet casing works fine. Just place the open end on the spot where you need to punch a hole and strike the other end with a hammer. You can have holes of all sizes depending on the caliber of rifles you or your friends own. Make sure you use an empty cartridge; you don't need to put a hole through the floor, too.

— *Gary Vorhes*
Peyton, Colorado

Boot Bird House

Hanger

Roof

Entrance

Perch

OLD WORN-OUT boots you're going to throw away can be put to better use. It's easy to make them into unique bird houses. My bird houses have housed cactus wrens for several years. Visitors are delighted at the unusual sight of a boot hanging in my tree, with birds coming and going.

Here's how to make one: Cut a 3-inch hole in the side of the upper boot top. Create the perch by making tiny holes with the tip of a knife; then insert a short stick. Make a roof from two boards nailed together.

Here's an even simpler way. I found an old discarded metal sign that measured 4 by 18 inches. After drilling two holes in the middle, I bent the sign at a 90-degree angle. Then I ran a coat hanger through the boot loops and the holes in the sign. The hanger serves dual purposes. It keeps the roof on the boot and makes it easy to hang in a tree.

— *Gary D. Kirchmeier*
Cave Creek, Arizona

Hat Hanger

I'VE FOUND an easy and inexpensive way to hang up your cowboy hat, especially if you're like me and have a half-dozen hats lying around that are getting stepped on, sat on and knocked aside. Take a wire coat hanger and bend it into a diamond shape, as shown. Put the crown of a hat through the hanger. Now you can hang it anywhere, and it'll be out of the way.

— *Edward M. Gray*
Cologne, Minnesota

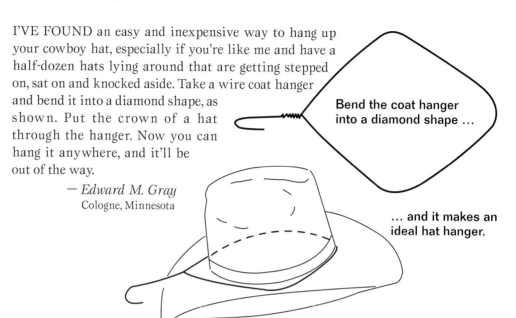

Bend the coat hanger into a diamond shape ...

... and it makes an ideal hat hanger.

Detangling Tails

"ALL THE BROODMARES we've sold have come right off the pasture, so I've had a lot of practice getting knots out of tails," says Linda Griffin of Coalinga, Calif.

Remember the old method of running a pocketknife down the middle to split the knot in half, then salvaging what was left? Linda says to forget that!

The Griffins put 2 cups of Absorbine ShowSheen into a small bucket. Then they push the tail into the bucket, with the knot being pushed firmly to the bottom and "squished around in the ShowSheen. Make sure you saturate the knot clear to its center," says Linda.

Don't do anything more with the tail for 2 days. The ShowSheen must dry completely so that there's no dampness even in the center of the knot. Made from a silicone base, the product "makes things slide better," says Linda, who adds that this method encourages hairs to separate from one another.

Comb with a dog-slicker brush, a wire grooming brush available from pet stores that carry dog-show supplies. Lynda prefers brushes by Warners.

"Start combing at the bottom of the tail, and work up," she instructs. "Because the slicker comb has a rectangular body, you can attack tough spots in the knot by pushing one corner of the brush deep into the area, then pulling it out. This will release several hairs."

Repeat this process, comb regularly, and you'll soon have the entire knot worked loose. Then, Linda says, "Thoroughly shampoo and rinse the tail; and apply conditioner." She likes to braid the tail because, after spending time in a knot, the tail tends to bush out like a kinky permanent wave. Braiding smooths it.

The Griffins have talked to other Paint Horse breeders and trainers who say they get the same knot-removal results by saturating the hair in fabric softener, which is also silicone-based. Whatever you use, Linda urges you to try this method and see how little hair is lost, compared to the old "pocketknife massacre."

— *Lynda Layne*
Winchester Bay, Oregon

117

Car Wash

ONE SIMPLE way to wash your horse is to take him to the car wash. Horses are usually a little bit hesitant the first time; but if you have a horse you can control well, you should be able to get him in the wash bay. I definitely don't recommend using the soap, only the rinse cycle. Car-wash soap dries a horse's skin and haircoat. Be cautious about holding the water wand too close to the horse. It operates with a lot of pressure, and if you get too close, the horse will soon let you know that it's hurting, rather than feeling good. The water is warm and almost has a massaging effect. Most horses take to it well.

Horses are usually frightened of drain grates at first, so try to avoid them. And make sure that if a horse does get excited, he can't get his foot caught in the grate.

Take your shovel and your rake, because inevitably the horse will leave little deposits. As a responsible horse owner, you should clean up after your horse.

— *Gene Naugle, D.V.M.*
Colorado Springs, Colorado

Reseating

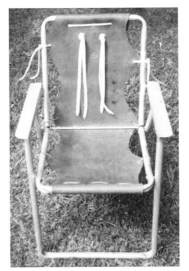

HERE'S A different approach to putting a new seat in an old lawn chair frame. Cut the leather to fit within the chair frame. Then punch holes along the leather's edge, and lace it onto the frame with rawhide.

— *W. Paul Brandt*
Mount Joy, Pennsylvania

One-Bale Hay Sled

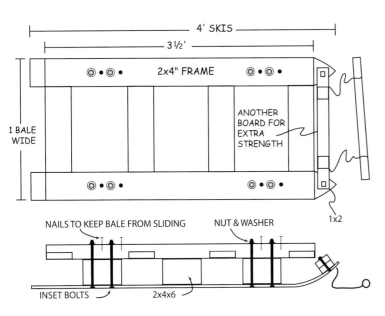

FEEDING HORSES in the winter can be quite a chore, especially if you have to hand-carry the bales. An easier method is this simple one-bale sled.

You'll need:
- 2 3½-foot 2-by-4s
- 4 1-by-4s (the width of a hay bale)
- 1 1-by-2 (the width of a hay bale)
- 1 1-foot length of broom handle
- 2 pieces of baling wire or rope
- 2 4-foot children's skis
- 6 2-by-4 by 6-inch blocks
- 12 7-inch bolts with nuts
- 2 1½-inch bolts with nuts
- A supply of 8- and 16-penny nails

This works better than a child's sled because the skis stay on top of the snow better than sled runners, and a bale stays put better than on a slick-surfaced sled.

— *Doris Platts*
Wilson, Wyoming

Rope Retrieval

WE OCCASIONALLY have a team-roping steer that's a little touchy about letting us take the rope off his heels. Two-foot catches are no problem, as the steer just steps out of the loop as the rope loosens. But when we catch only one hind foot on a steer that tends to kick, we have a little trick we use. We keep an iron rod with a small hook in the end at the stripping chute. This adds safety in this sometimes tricky operation.

Here's what to do: Stand on the same side of the steer that the rope is on; in other words, right foot, right side. Grab the steer's tail and pull him toward you to throw him off balance momentarily, then loosen the rope with the hook and let it fall off.

— Don Straight
DeSoto, Iowa

Chaps Adjustment

THE CHAPS that fit over your summer clothes provide good protection against snow and wind if you can get them fastened over your heavier-weight winter clothes. To adjust to the bigger sizes, my Dad, John Christensen, uses this method.

Tie a light cord to the bottom ring on your chaps and make a loop at each ring for the corresponding snap. At the top, punch a hole in the chap waistband, run the cord though the hole and knot it. After the initial adjustment, remove your chaps by unsnapping from the cord as if it was the ring. The cord stays with the chaps, attached at top and bottom. To put the chaps back on, poke a loop of cord through each ring and snap to it.

— Jan Guelff
Seeley Lake, Montana

Hay Hook Wire Cutter

I'VE SEEN SEVERAL ideas on how to cut wires and twine from hay bales. Wire cutters and pocketknives are sometimes hard to get at when wearing heavy winter gloves. In northern Iowa, we often feed hay on clean snow, and use a hay hook to drag it to the area we want to feed. I've found that by hooking the twine in the middle of the bale and giving it a couple of twists, it pops every time. But be sure to pick up and throw away the piece of twisted wire if it breaks off. If it stays in the hay, it could be swallowed by a horse or cow, resulting in "hardware" disease.

— *Don Straight*
Webster City, Iowa

Better Horn Wraps

HERE'S A TIP on additional horn protection for your roping cattle. Wrap your steer's horns with an Ace™ bandage, then follow up with your regular horn wraps. The Ace bandage helps to keep the steer from getting sore at the base of his horns and eliminates rope burns.

— *Wilbur Adank*
Hebron, Indiana

Sweatshirt Tailbag

THIS TAIL BAG is simple to make, and all you need is an old extra-large sweatshirt. Just follow these easy steps:

1. Cut sleeve from armpit and shoulder seam.
2. Cut along sleeve seam on left side to about 2 inches from the top.
3. Cut two more angled strips to the same distance from the top. If you've done this correctly, you should have three equal-width strips.
4. Turn sleeve inside out, and sew each strip into a tube, stitching just past the top and taking several backstitches.
5. Turn sleeve right side out.
6. Place tail inside armband. Stick a rubber-tipped bungie cord into the bottom of a tube, hook one-third of tail and pull through tube. Repeat on the remaining two tubes.
7. Braid the tubes, and secure a rubber band to bottom of bag.

This tail bag is great for pasture ponies.

— *Jo Schaef*
Hulett, Wyoming

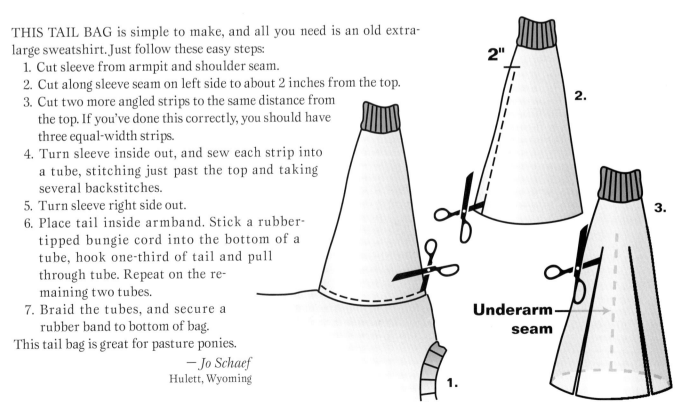

2"

2.

3.

Underarm seam

1.

Polish in a Pinch

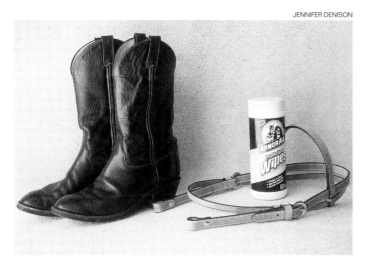

JENNIFER DENISON

BEFORE ENTERING the show, wipe off your boots and leather tack with a premoistened shoe-shining sponge (available at discount department stores for about $3). The sponge quickly removes dust, and is safe to use on almost all leather types and colors. Plus, it's easy to store in a garment bag, tack box or grooming tote.

Keep a container of Armor All® pop-up vinyl- or leather-conditioning wipes (designed for cleaning vehicle upholstery; available at discount department stores for about $5) in your tack box or grooming tote. They're great to quickly dust off or touch up your tack and boots. However, they shouldn't be a substitute for regular cleaning and conditioning.

— Jennifer Denison
Woodland Park, Colorado

Hook Danger

I'M WORRIED by hooks mounted in and around barns, stalls and even fences where horses are present because of the danger of a bridle, halter, rein or even a bit getting caught on one of them. In the years I've cowboyed I've seen a lot of damage done to horses and people when this happens.

My answer to the problem is simple and inexpensive. I make my hooks out of soft wire bent into the shape needed. This soft wire holds most light equipment, but also gives safely when things get western and a hang-up happens.

— Mike Papasan
Waldron, Arkansas

Inner Tubes

WE ACCIDENTALLY discovered something new to use when teaching a foal to lead. To give the foal something to play with, I'd thrown an old bicycle inner tube into his stall, with the valve stem cut out. When teaching the colt to lead, I picked up the inner tube, instead of using the usual rump rope. The inner tube is easier on the foal, has a wider base, and gives when the foal moves. Also, it's much easier on the handler's hands, and always provides a handhold. Now we're using it with our other foals. Another product recycled! My husband, a veterinarian, feels these inner tubes are safe for foals. As mentioned, we do remove the valve stems so they can't be chewed off and swallowed. We also throw larger tire inner tubes into paddocks for the foals to play with, which eases their boredom, and they sack out themselves, making it easier when the real sacking-out time comes. We have yet to have any foal or horses chew off a piece of the inner tube and swallow it. The tubes are too heavily walled, I think, and we also use tubes that are in relatively good condition.

— Marilyn Cerniga
Porterville, California

121

INDEX

NOTES

Western Horseman, established in 1936, is the world's leading horse publication. For subscription information: 800-877-5278. To order other *Western Horseman* books: 800-874-6774. *Western Horseman*, Box 7980, Colorado Springs, CO 80933-7980. Web site: **www.westernhorseman.com**.

Books Published by *Western Horseman*

ARABIAN LEGENDS by Marian K. Carpenter
280 pages and 319 photographs. Abu Farwa, *Aladdinn, *Ansata Ibn Halima, *Bask, Bay-Abi, Bay El Bey, Bint Sahara, Fadjur, Ferzon, Indraff, Khemosabi, *Morafic, *Muscat, *Naborr, *Padron, *Raffles, *Raseyn, *Sakr, Samtyr, *Sanacht, *Serafix, Skorage, *Witez II, Xenophonn.

BACON & BEANS by Stella Hughes
144 pages and 200-plus recipes for delicious western chow.

BARREL RACING, Completely Revised by Sharon Camarillo
128 pages, 158 photographs, and 17 illustrations. Teaches foundation horsemanship and barrel racing skills for horse and rider, with additional tips on feeding, hauling and winning.

CALF ROPING by Roy Cooper
144 pages and 280 photographs covering roping and tying.

CUTTING by Leon Harrel
144 pages and 200 photographs. Complete guide on this popular sport.

FIRST HORSE by Fran Devereux Smith
176 pages, 160 black-and-white photos, about 40 illustrations. Step-by-step information for the first-time horse owner and/or novice rider.

IMPRINT TRAINING by Robert M. Miller, D.V.M.
144 pages and 250 photographs. Learn to "program" newborn foals.

LEGENDS by Diane C. Simmons
168 pages and 214 photographs. Barbra B, Bert, Chicaro Bill, Cowboy P-12, Depth Charge (TB), Doc Bar, Go Man Go, Hard Twist, Hollywood Gold, Joe Hancock, Joe Reed P-3, Joe Reed II, King P-234, King Fritz, Leo, Peppy, Plaudit, Poco Bueno, Poco Tivio, Queenie, Quick M Silver, Shue Fly, Star Duster, Three Bars (TB), Top Deck (TB), and Wimpy P-1.

LEGENDS 2 by Jim Goodhue, Frank Holmes, Phil Livingston, Diane C. Simmons
192 pages and 224 photographs. Clabber, Driftwood, Easy Jet, Grey Badger II, Jessie James, Jet Deck, Joe Bailey P-4 (Gonzales), Joe Bailey (Weatherford), King's Pistol, Lena's Bar, Lightning Bar, Lucky Blanton, Midnight, Midnight Jr, Moon Deck, My Texas Dandy, Oklahoma Star, Oklahoma Star Jr., Peter McCue, Rocket Bar (TB), Skipper W, Sugar Bars, and Traveler.

LEGENDS 3 by Jim Goodhue, Frank Holmes, Diane Ciarloni, Kim Guenther, Larry Thornton, Betsy Lynch
208 pages and 196 photographs. Flying Bob, Hollywood Jac 86, Jackstraw (TB), Maddon's Bright Eyes, Mr Gun Smoke, Old Sorrel, Piggin String (TB), Poco Lena, Poco Pine, Poco Dell, Question Mark, Quo Vadis, Royal King, Showdown, Steel Dust, and Two Eyed Jack.

LEGENDS 4
216 pages and 216 photographs. Several authors chronicle the great Quarter Horses Zantanon, Ed Echols, Zan Parr Bar, Blondy's Dude, Diamonds Sparkle, Woven Web/Miss Princess, Miss Bank, Rebel Cause, Tonto Bars Hank, Harlan, Lady Bug's Moon, Dash For Cash, Vandy, Impressive, Fillinic, Zippo Pine Bar, and Doc O' Lena.

LEGENDS 5 by Frank Holmes, Ty Wyant, Alan Gold, and Sally Harrison
248 pages, including about 300 photographs. The stories of Little Joe, Joe Moore, Monita, Bill Cody, Joe Cody, Topsail Cody, Pretty Buck, Pat Star Jr., Skipa Star, Hank H, Chubby, Bartender, Leo San, Custus Rastus (TB), Jaguar, Jackie Bee, Chicado V and Mr Bar None.

PROBLEM-SOLVING by Marty Marten
248 pages and over 250 photos and illustrations. How to develop a willing partnership between horse and human to handle trailer-loading, hard-to-catch, barn-sour, spooking, water-crossing, herd-bound, and pull-back problems.

NATURAL HORSE-MAN-SHIP by Pat Parelli
224 pages and 275 photographs. Parelli's six keys to a natural horse-human relationship.

REINING, Completely Revised by Al Dunning
216 pages and over 300 photographs showing how to train horses for this exciting event.

RODEO LEGENDS by Gavin Ehringer
Photos and life stories fill 216 pages. Included are: Joe Alexander, Jake Barnes & Clay O'Brien Cooper, Joe Beaver, Leo Camarillo, Roy Cooper, Tom Ferguson, Bruce Ford, Marvin Garrett, Don Gay, Tuff Hedeman, Charmayne James, Bill Linderman, Larry Mahan, Ty Murray, Dean Oliver, Jim Shoulders, Casey Tibbs, Harry Tompkins, and Fred Whitfield.

ROOFS AND RAILS by Gavin Ehringer
144 pages, 128 black-and-white photographs plus drawings, charts, and floor plans. How to plan and build your ideal horse facility.

STARTING COLTS by Mike Kevil
168 pages and 400 photographs. Step-by-step process in starting colts.

THE HANK WIESCAMP STORY by Frank Holmes
208 pages and over 260 photographs. The biography of the legendary breeder of Quarter Horses, Appaloosas and Paints.

TEAM PENNING by Phil Livingston
144 pages and 200 photographs. How to compete in this popular family sport.

TEAM ROPING WITH JAKE AND CLAY by Fran Devereux Smith
224 pages and over 200 photographs and illustrations. Learn about fast times from champions Jake Barnes and Clay O'Brien Cooper. Solid information about handling a rope, roping dummies, and heading and heeling for practice and in competition. Also sound advice about rope horses, roping steers, gear and horsemanship.

WELL-SHOD by Don Baskins
160 pages, 300 black-and-white photos and illustrations. A horseshoeing guide for owners and farriers. The easy-to-read text, illustrations, and photos show step-by-step how to trim and shoe a horse for a variety of uses. Special attention is paid to corrective shoeing techniques for horses with various foot and leg problems.

WESTERN HORSEMANSHIP by Richard Shrake
144 pages and 150 photographs. Complete guide to riding western horses.

WESTERN TRAINING by Jack Brainard
With Peter Phinny. 136 pages. Stresses the foundation for western training.

WIN WITH BOB AVILA by Juli S. Thorson
This 128-page, hardbound, full-color book discusses traits that separate horse-world achievers from also-rans. World champion horseman Bob Avila shares his philosophies on succeeding as a competitor, breeder, and trainer.